MONICA ZUNNY
*INTERNATIONAL SPEAKER &
RELATIONSHIP INTELLIGENCE COACH*

How to
Make It Work
When Love Is Not
Enough

A HELP IN TIMES WHEN MARRIAGE HURTS

How to Make it Work

WHEN LOVE IS NOT ENOUGH

Monica Zunny

CONTENTS

DEDICATION

This book is dedicated to that couple currently going through turbulence in their marriage, and you are determined to do the will of God and keep your marriage. May God strengthen you and grant you wisdom and understanding to deal in the affairs of your marriage to the praise and glory of God. May you find grace to help in times when marriage hurts.

ACKNOWLEDGEMENTS

I am a product of many lessons.

My praise and gratitude go to the lover of my soul, my Lord and Saviour Jesus Christ, for His many graces in my life and for bringing me this far. Thank you, Holy Spirit of grace, for the inner nudges and the leading you give, my extraordinary strategist and best friend; I adore you, Lord.

I am eternally grateful to my father, life coach and pastor, Reverend Dr Chris Oyakhilome Dsc, Dsc, DD. Growing up in the Loveworld Nation for the past thirty-plus years is one of the greatest blessings of my life.

To my husband, legendary PZA, you have invested a lot in me over the twenty-plus years of our marriage. I pray for better days with you. My children are the best, Chris-Rhema and Chris-Mimshach; mummy loves you both for the hype and calms you mix into the art of living for me.

My dear mother and mother-in-law, your lives are milestones in this marriage journey; your counsel, unconditional love, and prayers keep me going.

To every woman, man, and couple I have had the opportunity to counsel and help in the journey of their marriage and relationship through Relationship Intelligence and Positive Marriage Initiative, may God continue to bless your home.

To the great team at Relationship Intelligence and Positive Marriage Initiative, you are beyond amazing. May God bless you all.

INTRODUCTION

What Was Your Idea of a Great Marriage?

Love is a powerful tool for building relationships; love can cut across tribes and tongues, pulling down cultural walls and educational boundaries. Love becomes the bedrock on which many relationships metamorphose into marriage, which is a great mystery to some who may never understand how two people with seemingly different backgrounds, social statuses, and physical differences end up in love.

Yet two people can get married without defining their love- because love can be built with time and other important values make love work. As beautiful as love seems, it is important to know that sometimes love cannot sustain a marriage.

Terms and Conditions Apply

Every relationship is premised on something that ignites the attention of those involved, which blossoms into what we eventually describe as love when nurtured. In my opinion, that is the terms and conditions on which the relationship exists, and when it is allowed to thrive, blossom and flourish, it can develop into marriage. As people become familiar with and get used to themselves, these terms and conditions may evolve into other forms of terms and conditions, which is an unwritten code of understanding and tolerance.

Problems begin when these codes are broken, compromised, or disrespected. And then people begin to fall out of love in their marriage. Some couples start out professing love for each other and still say they love each other but are unwilling to continue as a couple in their marriage due to failed expectations.

To solve the problem, we must go back to the foundation of the relationship and re-appraise the terms and conditions. Unfortunately, these may not have been written or even acknowledged in the first place. This is one of the reasons I advocate that people must engage in meaningful conversations and ask the right questions during dating and courtship. You are awakened to why they choose to love and marry you by doing so.

In this book, you will find important information on how to identify, understand and navigate the different paths in marriage to help you take the reins of your marriage and make the best of it.

One thing you must bear in mind is that every marriage is unique as much as the individuals are unique; while there are universally accepted codes of conduct in marriage, the uniqueness and individuality of the people involved make it necessary to also apply these codes to certain degrees in the different and unique marriages; that is as unique and personal as it gets.

No matter how we are admonished to love our neighbour as ourselves, we may not be able to marry and live with every neighbour under the same roof as we do with the individual to whom we may be married. Yet, in a unique twist, if and when we choose to give some attention to that neighbour, it may be possible to understand their personality deeply enough to ignite a subtle liking, and as we open up to conversations with them, chances are, that the possibility that we may begin to love them gets even higher. This love, even if first called agape, can metamorphose into something more romantic and engaging, and the rest may be history.

Humans are predominantly love beings, though many have been conditioned to give and receive love differently by their upbringing, situation, circumstances, and many other factors.

When we make an effort to understand our God, ourselves, our relationships with people, and the world we live in, with the right information, we can all blossom into a better version of ourselves and be able to live for a course, love genuinely, aspire to something bigger than us and thrive in all our endeavours; this will culminate into a fulfilled and purposeful life which will benefit you and those who cross your path- this, in a nutshell, is what Relationship Intelligence is about. From that standpoint, we now share our thoughts with you.

We will tell stories at some point to help us drive home our proposed values. We hope you find this book as interesting as it was for us to write.

The Four Cardinal points

Many things come to mind in this journey of marriage. Often, in the cycle of every marriage, there may be challenges that concern four cardinal points

1. Faith
2. Family
3. Finances
4. Fidelity

Many other important issues will arise from these that may lead to a solid or broken marriage. Our expectations or the lack of expectations in marriage are critical foundations on which we build our marriage, which can make or break it for us.

One theme you will find throughout this book is that marriage is a decision you make, and you can always count on God's word to furnish you with ample wisdom and grace for the race.

It takes two to get married, but it only requires one person to break that union, as significant as the vows to live together forever is; one person who decides that they are no longer willing to be a part of that sacred vow to live together forever can pull down the whole structure of that marriage no matter how long it may have been standing.

As you read this book, we hope that your decision to strengthen your marriage and work things out is fueled by every thought we communicate in this book. We will also tell stories using the lives and choices of Damien and Janelle and, in other chapters, highlight the facts we have garnered from different scenarios.

As you follow the thoughts expressed in this book, it is hoped that on the journey to building the marriage/home of your dreams, you see that navigating the twists and turns in marriage requires much more than paying lip service to the word LOVE- Love requires work and sacrifices yet it must be the premise on which we take all actions in the love walk called marriage.

What, then, is love? How do you define love? Up until now, I have found no better definition than the one I heard from a man of God, and here it is

"Love is that endearing value of a person that gives you a sense of his or her importance to you." this is the definition from Pastor Chris Oyakhilome.

Love is endearing; it is a doing word, active and not passive. This love from above is pure and then very easy to entreat; it does not keep a record of wrong done. This is the true love that God gives, and God has given us the capacity to give others, and no one is more deserving of this love than the one you married.

With the above in mind, I would appreciate it if you could close your eyes and recall your expectations of marriage and if every moment of your journey in marriage has been fulfilling. If not, what are you willing to do to change that narrative? But if you are unmarried, you can still think deeply about how you have built any valid expectations and how realistic they may be if you went into marriage holding those expectations dear to your heart. When we truly love the one we marry, all our expectations will align with God's expectations, plans, and His word. Then only will love be truly enough for us and work through us to that place of bliss. If we truly see our spouse as valuable to God, enough to endear God to place such value on us and allow Jesus Christ to die for us. That is how important you are to God and how valuable you are to God. Why should you live with someone who has no value for you, all in the name of love? It is a misunderstanding and misuse of such an important word-LOVE.

We strongly recommend that you make your notes and checklist from each chapter, and we have included a sample template to guide you in doing so.

Whatever the state of your marriage at the point where you are reading this book, we pray and hope that you find this book helpful in your journey to strengthen your marriage and enjoy better days ahead.

God bless you.

1

UNDERSTANDING THE PURPOSE OF MARRIAGE.

Many people may have heard how man was created in the Garden of Eden, and God said it is not good for man to be alone. I will make a help meet for him, and God made a woman and gave the woman to the man who called her Eve. So, it was Adam and Eve that God made.

From there, we see there was a purpose for marriage. Even though there was no formal ceremony, the purpose was defined. God made marriage to fulfil these three main purposes, which, by extension, flow into some other things.

A. Companionship/Communion/Fellowship
B. Productivity- Material and Procreation
C. Pleasure-communication/warmth

Let us examine the purpose listed above closely

A. Companionship/Communion/Fellowship

God said it is not good for man to be alone; being alone and being lonely are two different things, again because of the purpose of procreation that God had set on the course every creature was to procreate according to its kind-kindred. There was no other creature in the likeness of the man, Adam, who was made in the likeness of God, so there would be a likeness in form, reasoning, and appearance.

This would make companionship relatable and humane, leading to bonding and fellowship and creating a purposeful endearment.

There will then be a communion-koinonia between Adam and Eve and ultimately with God and man(humans), which is premised on the fact that God made them- man and woman in His likeness, created He them- male and female, and this communion would lead to fellowship; fellowship is a solid part of man, whom God made in His image so He-God can fellowship with man in a relationship that is of reasonable value and content.

God would come in the cool of the day to fellowship with Adam; this was customary, and with that custom, it was easy for God to detect that something was wrong early enough in His relationship with the man. God had come to fellowship with the man as His custom was, and here the man was hiding, so God called out to Adam, Adam, where are you? The answer was, "I heard your voice walking in the garden, and so I hid because I was naked."…

You know the rest of the story. This highlights the place of fellowship in marriage; you must be in constant fellowship with your spouse, and a rich and bountiful fellowship can help strengthen your marriage. Then, you will be able to notice early enough when an intruder sneaks in to sow seeds of discord and doubt.

No matter how busy or tired you may be, find time for fellowship and be in constant communication and communion as much as possible.

Talk about it; I mean anything and everything that matters to you as individuals and as a couple. Be caring, discerning, empathetic, and genuinely loving.

When on a trip or in a long-distance marriage for whatever reasons, make fellowship a priority; this will enrich your communion and make up for companionship to some extent, as much as you can; a day should not go by without you talking. This may require a lot of effort as there may be challenges with differences in time zones and other problems, so the required effort must be put in to make it happen.

B. Productivity- Material and Procreation

Adam- Man, awoke to full creation, and God had finished all the work of creation; this, for me, is very profound as it speaks volumes- it connotes that every man has a job prepared for him to do on this earth before he is born. If you allow God to guide you, you will not need to search too deep or go too far to find your calling. The reason you were born is inside you, and you will find it when you begin your walk with God.

Interestingly, God had confidence in the man He created to continue the work of creation; Adam had the responsibility of naming all the animals that God created, which is powerful; a lot of intelligence comes into play there. So, man was given the charge to manage his world, the garden of Eden where he was born and where he lived; Eden had all the resources that man would need for food, sustainability, growth, and productivity materially, financially, and relationship-wise which includes food for all the other creatures.

Then, God made a woman fit for Adam for fellowship, procreation, and the work he was given to do, which was to maintain and keep the garden and all that was on the earth. I think God made Eve after He had created Adam and given him his Job Description and Terms of Reference because He didn't want there to be assumptions as to whose role it was to do what, so Eve had to take her Job Description from Adam, that speaks of boundaries, delegation, supervision, leadership and headship.

I think God made Eve after He had created Adam and given him his Job Description and Terms of Reference because He didn't want there to be assumptions as to whose role it was to do what, so Eve had to take her Job Description from Adam, that speaks of boundaries, delegation, supervision, leadership and headship.

With the guarantee of a home, the next meal, and much more, there is room for warmth and relaxation after a day at work; there is room for deliberation and feedback. There may be disagreements and deferring opinions, but we always agree to friendship, companionship, and fellowship. So, in the midst of all, there is time for romance, which gives rise to pleasure and from pleasure, we can also procreate. I believe marriage is to accomplish several things, including Companionship, Pleasure, and Procreation.

C. Pleasure-communication/warmth

Truly, the purpose for which God made man and woman as husband and wife is intertwined. In the place of work- productivity, there is interaction, and skills are brought into play, which may ignite admiration and spark conversations. It is so important that people get busy with their life's calling before they even think of getting married. That's where true fulfilment comes, and that is where your authentic self can blossom.

It is so important that people get busy with their life's calling before they even think of getting married. That's where true fulfilment comes, and that is where your authentic self can blossom.

Living Is for Impact

Life is not truly lived until it touches other lives, and you can impact lives with the fruits of your very existence, which is why God brought you into this world in the first place. In this purpose of marriage, taking your place gives room for interactions, and there lies pleasure, too. Man and Woman, humans generally by their very nature, are wired for love, but this love must be in the right order:

    a. Love God
    b. Love yourself, your neighbour as yourself, And the person you marry, just as Christ loved the church and gave Himself for the church.
    c. Love life, every moment of it, the highs and lows, make the pudding a good meal.

You only live once, make the best of living, and as much as you can, make room in your space for others to live their best life, too.

Create, make, and find pleasure in your marriage. Over time, I have realised that many things in life result from the choices we make consciously or unconsciously. To resign yourself to fate is an unconscious choice to accept whatever comes to you. But you can still choose to be happy and find pleasure in the simple everyday things that make up the totality of your life.

Marriage is where we must intentionally make room for pleasure, laughter, fulfilment, friendship, and joy. It's a choice, and one of the secrets is to give one hundred per cent and expect nothing in return.

Whatever happens, set boundaries, define your threshold, and put yourself in perspective. It is important to look out for your spouse and give it your best and your all, but don't lose yourself; stay in the picture and take your place at the table. Many people work so hard to make dinner and keep working while dinner is served, and while everyone is at the dinner table, they're still running around serving tables and ensuring everyone is fine.

They never really take their place at the table and are satisfied eating leftovers.

Whether you are the man of the house making the money to put food on the table or you are the woman of the house cooking the meals and ensuring everyone is served, never discount yourself from the equation called everybody; ensure you take your hands off the running around and take your place at the table when dinner is served to eat your meal and take a good portion too. (I am not talking about literally eating dinner, but being present in the things that matter in your home and making sure you eat from of the fruits of your labour) Often people are treated the way they present themselves and you will be addressed how you dress and show up. Show up for you and your loved ones. Show up for your gender and your pack at home, work, and the universe. You only live once.

> **Often people are treated the way they present themselves and you will be addressed how you dress and show up. Show up for you and your loved ones. Show up for your gender and your pack at home, work, and the universe. You only live once.**

This thing called marriage is like a building; God has given us the prototype, but we all can choose to determine the kind of building we want. One important thing about building a house is that there must be a foundation, which, even though not seen outwardly, determines the final structure and how long the house will stand.

You cannot have a foundation for a bungalow and then put on it a three or four-floor building; it will come down at some point. You must have conversations (even before marriage) to determine the kind of structure you want in your marriage; a lot of people go into marriage with expectations and assumptions that their spouse should know what to do and think that it is a given that a lady or a man should handle certain issues in a particular manner because it was part of their upbringing or their parents handled such issues this way or that way.

These expectations and assumptions have mostly been the greatest undoing for many marriages. The disappointment and shock that many experience when they find out how far apart their expectations and reality are is even more challenging for many to deal with, to the point that they never even try to work things out in their marriage when challenges come.

I must state this very early in this book: always make room for explanations and make excuses for your spouse while working on your marriage. You must keep the communication lines open at all times and never conclude a matter until you have heard the other person out. We must always make every effort not to judge people by their actions, as we often judge ourselves by our intentions, so we must open the communication lines to allow others to tender an explanation for their actions and understand their intentions from there.

We must always make every effort not to judge people by their actions, as we often judge ourselves by our intentions, so we must open the communication lines to allow others to tender an explanation for their actions and understand their intentions from there.

One thing to avoid is to conclude a matter reported to you about your spouse without hearing their side of the story. No matter what the situation is, as long as the people around you know that you have shut the communication lines between you and your spouse, they will tell you things that probably never happened or report a matter to you in a way that will make you hold your spouse in contempt, especially those who never really liked the person, or who think that it will be pleasing to you. The Best approach is never to conclude until you have spoken to your spouse, no matter where you are in your relationship. Remember, you are married and have become one flesh, and anything you do or say against that person has a ripple effect that comes back to you.

The Best approach is never to conclude until you have spoken to your spouse, no matter where you are in your relationship. Remember, you are married and have become one flesh, and anything you do or say against that person has a ripple effect that comes back to you.

Have you noticed that couples who love themselves begin to look alike? So it is with fighting couples they look alike because emotions and feelings run deeper than the surface or flesh, and the one flesh syndrome binds them spiritually and creates a picture of their deepest thoughts and feelings for each other.

Truly, what is the colour of love? Love or hatred reflects in the mirror of your marriage if that is the predominant emotion you feel for each other. Because life and death are in the power of your tongue, and as you speak and talk about your spouse in good or bad terms, the material of your words produces results in your Marriage, good or bad.

Be mindful of words; they make or mare you and all that concerns you, and they are spirits; once voiced, it becomes difficult, if not impossible, to take it back.

 Learn to speak blessings at all times, as it concerns your marriage, and put yourself in your spouse's place to see how well you can take those words and what they produce in you.

Making the best decisions and taking actions in the best interest of our lives as individuals and in the best interest of our vow, commitments, and faith, as we promised, is a critical part of building a good marriage. Sometimes, these decisions and actions may be hurtful to our partners and us, but in the long haul, they work for us with a far more eternal weight of glory as we keep the bond of fellowship within the boundaries of God's word that a man should love his wife as himself and a woman should see to it that she submits to her husband as the bible puts it in the book of **Ephesians 5:28-33(AMPC)**

Even so, husbands should love their wives as [being in a sense] their own bodies. He who loves his own wife loves himself. For no man ever hated his own flesh, but nourishes and carefully pro-tects and cherishes it, as Christ does the church. Because we are members (parts) of His body. For this reason, a man shall leave his father and his mother and shall be joined to his wife, and the two shall become one flesh. This mystery is very great, but I speak concerning [the relation of] Christ and the church. However, let each man of you [without exception] love his wife as [being in a

> *sense] his very own self; and let the wife see that she respects and reverences her husband [that she notices him, regards him, honors him, prefers him, venerates, and esteems him; and that she defers to him, praises him, and loves and admires him exceedingly].*
> ***Ephesians 5:28-33***

Indeed, you should read the whole of Ephesians chapter five to understand to some extent the sacrifices you have to make in marriage, which is not cumbersome if we choose to walk with the Holy Spirit because He is the only one who can teach us to love. Many do not even know how to love themselves and how much more to love others. Here in lies the most important work. We cannot give what we don't have, and we must learn to love ourselves and understand ourselves before we can love someone else, even the one we marry.

> **Many do not even know how to love themselves and how much more to love others. Here in lies the most important work. We cannot give what we don't have, and we must learn to love ourselves and understand ourselves before we can love someone else, even the one we marry.**

Many marry the one they love, but you must continue to love the one you marry; this is where the work is, regardless of what you saw that attracted you to the one you marry; when you are married, even when you see something else, you must convince yourself to love the one you married.

To know, understand and be able to love, we must allow God's overflowing love to permeate and fill us to overflow; only from that point can we love anyone else. I pray that we all get to that point where we have loved God deeply enough to believe His every word and then yield ourselves to the Holy Spirit to help us live the word of God in every area of our lives, even concerning marriage.

On this note, I submit that sometimes love is not enough, for the love that is professed and not put into action is not enough. We must drop our pride, ego, insecurities, and culture, submit to God and His word in our marriage, and let Him work His ideal love. We must constantly be in fellowship and deeply in love with the God of our salvation, who understands us, understands and knows everyone, and has excess love for all humans. When we do so, God will fill us with more than enough to love ourselves regardless of our frailties and love others despite their shortcomings.

Yet, as we genuinely love the one we marry, we see that love is not enough to sustain any relationship because in our love walk, there are sacrifices we must make, there are choices we must make, there are obligations in our commitments, and even if we mean well, sometimes the pressures of life and other interests can derail us from our commitment. We must seek to acknowledge at all times that we are committed to our commitments.

Yet, the discipline to stay when the one you married is pleased to dwell with you, the tenacity and staying power just because you love God and do not want to break His word on the excuse that they lied to you about something and that has shattered your expectations. The conviction to stay true to your vows despite all is really what love is. So when we find that love is not enough- our human and limited love, we must then draw on love- God's abundant love, to find what is missing and make the best of the decisions we made to love one another even as Christ loved the church and gave himself for her. This is the purpose and fulfilment of marriage, as God planned it from the beginning.

ACTION NOTE/CHECKLIST

1. Always keep the communication lines open and give feedback. Communication is the oxygen that keeps relationships going.

2. Marriage requires attention; be intentional and deliberately work it out; unlike dating or courtship, you can't walk out and walk in as you please at any time. You stay the course and work it out

3. Trust is the foundation of any thriving relationship. Please do not break it or withdraw it. No marriage can work without trust

8. Love is a choice more than a force. Love your spouse even in times of trials and differences. Only then can you resolve any issue. But by all means, do not attempt to stay and resolve an issue that jeopardises your physical, mental, and spiritual health and well-being.

PRAYER

Dear Heavenly Father, I ask that you grant me the wisdom to deal wisely with my marriage and help me stay true to my vows.

In Jesus Matchless Name- Amen

God bless you, and I love you.

PERSONAL RESOLUTION /EXERCISE

Are there any areas in your life or marriage that you need to take action on due to what you learned? Kindly document your thoughts, resolutions, and actions. Writing them down is a powerful way of documenting them in your mind so you can remember to take action.

Start by writing at least three key things concerning your thoughts, resolutions, and corresponding actions.

Thoughts

1.______________________________________

2______________________________________

3______________________________________

Resolutions

1______________________________________

2.______________________________________

3______________________________________

Action to be taken

1______________________________________

2______________________________________

3______________________________________

2

THE MAN IN MARRIAGE

The man is the head of the union, the husband of the wife is the head of the house, the boss and king, and must be treated as a king at all times. Every man who is the husband of a wife has a territory to protect and provide for. Beginning with your wife, a new nation has begun, headed by the man who is the husband. That is why the Bible says:

"Therefore shall a man leave his father and his mother, and shall cleave unto his wife: and they shall be one flesh"
Genesis 2:24

This is both an instruction and a law in the sense of its finality. In many cultures, the woman leaves her father and mother to marry her husband, both physically and emotionally, in a sense. But the man must leave too; it is more important for the man to leave, or else the new nation may never be fully born.

This man, who is this wife's husband, is not continuing his father's lineage, but he is starting a fresh walk with God; the most important separation must occur in the mind, spirit, and body. This man must have jurisdiction and a boundary for his household. He must have a definite, clear location called home and a definite, clear assignment, which is his job, and wake up to something meaningful and productive, even if he were a prince or king.

The man is a whole being, rational and emotional, having reasoning and possessing balls between his legs; he is not the head of every female because he is a man, so he cannot go around lording it over all the females in his space, from his mother to his sisters, female colleagues, female friends and every other lady around. He is only the head of the woman he is married to.

This is what it means to be the head, but what is a head without a body? You bet you don't want to imagine that- it will be some form of horrifying being, so as the head moves, he carries his body along, and that presents some form of completeness; the body cannot have a mind of its own, the body has to go where the head goes and do the biddings of the head but if the head keeps making wrong judgments, the whole entity will soon get into some trouble and may even become sick.

Most men are more rational than women in their approach to life, love, and many matters. They live in compartments; by this, I mean they can focus on one thing at a time. For example, if a man who loves soccer (football) is watching a football match, all his attention and emotions are focused on that match at that time.

That is one of the reasons women should deal with their husbands with wisdom. I heard of a case where a man had thrown his wife from the first floor of a building downstairs because she wanted his attention while he was watching a football match, and she turned off the TV set instead, which enraged him.

For all good intent, I am not justifying this act; those who do this kind of thing have not learned to manage their emotions, and there are consequences.

Because of the ability to compartmentalise, some men can be going through a crisis in their marriage and still be hitting their targets and goals at work. Also, some men may be having an extramarital affair and still make their wives happy as long as, in their opinion, the wife is respectful, dutiful, loving, and obedient. They feel they did not go into the affair to spite nor replace their wife. Except, of course, the extra begins to manipulate them.

Note, I'm not talking about the rightness or wrongness of these things but their very existence inside life.

The Bible is clear about who the man is in marriage; in Christian marriage, the man is the head and the boss; that's how crystal clear it can be; this position has responsibilities and obligations, and as the husband, he is to love his wife and protect her even at the expense of his life if it requires it. That is what it means to be a husband. He is to provide for her and his household; otherwise, he is even described as being worse than an infidel, a word used to describe an unbeliever; he is termed a worse specimen of a man if he fails in his responsibility to provide for his family which includes his wife because even the unbeliever provides for his family.

> *But if any provide not for his own, especially for those of his own house, he hath denied the faith and is worse than an infidel.*
> **1 Timothy 5:8**

This is the reality; it is a matter of divine instruction that a man should provide for his family and that responsibility he must accept and discharge regardless of how much money his wife has or makes. A man who is planning with his wife's money has automatically denied the faith and, by so doing, makes the word of God of non affect his life in that area.

> **When you refuse the responsibilities that come with headship, you automatically short-circuit the grace for ahead-ship. The God who made you the head knows you can handle it, so you work on being the head, and the grace of having will follow.**

When you refuse the responsibilities that come with headship, you automatically short-circuit the grace for ahead-ship. The God who made you the head knows you can handle it, so you work on being the head, and the grace of having will follow.

I hope we will understand the principles of God's word governing marriage. The husband is to love his wife with understanding; this is very important, as it can make the difference between night and day. Your wife is not the girlfriend you married; your wife is not the mother or sister you grew up with. This individual of the female human species is unique and must be understood to be loved.

Some profound authors have done well to give us revelations about Love Language and personality types. It is important to understand your wife's love language and personality type. You also need to understand her background- spiritually and, indeed, all other areas of her life.

Understand your wife as an individual; you may need to study her like a book and make notes of the different aspects where you may find some differences that will help you love her better and relate with her in a way that will bring out the best in her.

Your wife is your garden; nurture her and plant the right seeds so that you can harvest them in good time. You must understand her as a soil and know the seeds that will best produce the right harvest in her. It is the farmer who has the responsibility to understand the soil and know how to irrigate it for the best harvest.

Some soils are fallow grounds; you have to keep cultivating them and plant seasonal crops to break them and condition them before you plant trees in them because trees need depth to flourish. I can hear someone thinking what exactly do you mean?

Well, you must invest in your wife as a man, but such investments must be made based on your understanding of your wife, her capacity (which, of course, can be improved on), and all other characteristics.

For example, it may not be very profitable to insist that a woman does business when she is cut out for a career. Some women may be good at managing money, while others may not be so good at that. So instead of giving her some funds to go and invest and expecting returns, you may as well invest the money on her behalf, maybe by buying a piece of land in her name and banking it for a good time to resell and make a profit. Identify and strengthen her strengths, de-emphasise her weaknesses, or complement her weaknesses with your strengths. Also, discussing her weakness with a third party is unnecessary. Just ensure you always have her back- that is integral to love.

As the husband of The wife you married, it will not be very healthy for your marriage if you act like a boss or mask-man before your wife. This will force her to create her impression of you and, by so doing, misrepresent you and what you stand for. Human beings are kindred by nature, and it will help to share a kindred spirit with your spouse with genuine care, concern, and support for each other and what you most surely believe in or stand for.

Imagine a man who loves eating pounded yam at home, and when he shows up with his wife at a party, and she gets him pounded yam, he rejects it and asks for rice instead to appear unpredictable to everyone, including his wife. For him, this is a way of shielding himself against people who may be profiling him. It's just not okay. You make your wife uncomfortable and insecure, and then she loses confidence. Validate your wife as much as possible, boost her confidence, encourage her, and compliment her often. Remember, you picked her out of the many ladies you had the chance to be with or knew and chose her to walk beside you as your wife.

She is the one you officially agreed to live with, the one that calms your nerves when you are in the mood, and the mother of your children. (where applicable) please give her some honour and a place at the table.

We all live in different phases through life, and for the most part, after getting married, a lot of men focus on a career, which may be a business or a professional career; as much as you can as a man, let your wife into the important rudiments of your business, after all, a lot of men claim to be working so hard to give their spouse and children a better life and future.

Even when the business requires a certain skill set that your wife may not possess, you can invest in her by teaching her or sending her to training or something. This may be your best choice to carry your business to the next generation. While we are all praying for long life and prosperity, it may be in the best interest of all stakeholders to remember that life happens, and we are better prepared for anything than to be caught unaware.

We have seen a handful of men who met an untimely or unfortunate incident that left their wives and children in abject poverty and disarray. At the same time, they have laboured and left their fortune to the banks or strangers and some insensitive relatives. This may happen to a wife as well.

Husband, allow your wife to have financial independence and support her to flourish; allow her to have a career or a business. Do not seek to make her less than you met her before you married her- that, too, is a form of witchcraft. Your wife's success is your success, and that will not dull your shine. The level of your success can be evaluated by how your wife shows up; it directly reflects how you are performing your duty as a husband by providing for her and supporting her to shine in her space.

> The level of your success can be evaluated by how your wife shows up; it directly reflects how you are performing your duty as a husband by providing for her and supporting her to shine in her space.

If she can work for it and afford it, that takes the burden off you, but you must create the enabling environment for her; it will take the pressure off you, and that does not stop you from providing what you can afford. Nobody is asking you to rob a bank to provide for your family, but providing for your family, beginning with your wife should be a joy for you, even if she earns more than you earn. It's a principle that God put in place which brings to the husband a blessing directly consequent upon fulfilling it.

The husband should protect his wife in all ramifications, physically, emotionally, and materially and protect her against ill-treatment from in-laws and out-laws, as the case may be. In protecting her with respect, the husband is not permitted to talk his wife down at any time, whether in private or public or in the presence of the family or children.

ACTION NOTE/CHECKLIST

1. Respect is more valuable to a man in marriage than many things.

2. Understand the person you married and, as much as you can, make excuses for them

3. Do not hold grudges against each other; be quick to forgive and express yourself to your spouse.

4. Always give your spouse the opportunity for an explanation, and never take that for granted

5. Never use the silent treatment, maltreatment, violence, or verbal abuse against your spouse; remember, you have become one; anything you do against your spouse always finds its way back to you and with dividends

6. Sometimes, that is the reason for the frustrations that show up even in the most unlikely places, sometimes in your business or workplace or even as an ailment.

PRAYER

Dear heavenly Father, thank you for the many graces you've granted me; I trust you for more wisdom in dealing with my marriage and life to the praise and glory of God.

In Jesus matchless Name - *Amen*

Based On what you learned above, please write down three key things that concern your thoughts, resolutions, and corresponding actions.

Thoughts

1.____

2____

3____

Resolutions

1____

2.____

3____

Action to be taken

1____

2____

3____

3

THE WOMAN IN MARRIAGE

In His infinite wisdom, God decided to crown creation with the jewel called woman. This understanding will help many people appreciate the creation called a woman and, by extension, help the married man and woman place the right value on the different creations called man and woman. This is even more important in marriage; the man and the woman are creations made for different purposes yet complementary in their relationship as husband and wife. The woman is a helper, a warmer, a multiplier, an incubator of life and everything living, including dreams; she, as a wife, provides balance and some level of dependability for the husband, who is the head.

She cannot cut off the head by deciding on whatever she likes; remember, the brain, eyes, ears, nose, and mouth are all a part of the head; basically, four of the five senses are part of the head. But God put two important bodily senses- the hands and the heart.

So a woman is led by her heart and her feelings more like hands, while the man is led by his eyes and head, walking by sight, processing everything rationally, and if he saw it, then that is what it is; nobody can lie to him, he is not a fool, he saw it with his own eyes.

...While many men are more rational in their approach to love, most women are predominantly driven by emotions, that is, their hearts and feelings. The fact remains that sometimes it does not always make sense. This sometimes explains why a woman can remain in an abusive marriage for many years and keep making excuses for the man. This one is very disturbing: how can a man profess love for you and still turn around and beat you, and you believe it is love? In the same vein, a woman can be sexually molested by anybody, even a relative (incest), and she will still be committed to the person and still (love) the person. She believes the person loves her, and her sense of reasoning is skewed into the philosophy that love often comes at a price.

So, she believes anything the person tells her and accepts responsibility for the wrong part of it all; she may even blame God for making her a woman. A woman may be told it was her fault that she was raped because she is simply irresistible and hot, and she may accept that as a compliment and price it above the offence. What a life!

This ought not to be the description of the Christian woman who knows her worth and value and understands what it means to be the crowning jewel of God's creation. The woman is beautiful but not arrogant; you are fragile in your physical composition but not weak; there lies your strength. You are important to God, your world, and your family, even if they don't show it; that may be because they don't know it; you are interesting but not a plaything; you are delicately and fearfully and wonderfully made, and so should not be tampered with, experimented with nor used. Sometimes, it's nearly irreparable when a woman allows herself to be used, demeaned, disregarded, and wounded.

to God, your world, and your family, even if they don't show it; that may be because they don't know it; you are interesting but not a plaything; you are delicately and fearfully and wonderfully made, and so should not be tampered with, experimented with nor used. Sometimes, it's nearly irreparable when a woman allows herself to be used, demeaned, disregarded, and wounded.

But she is strong; the woman is one of the strongest creations that graced this earth. She can be so fragile and vulnerable but can be trusted with the most delicate factor that keeps life going on- a human fetus- the very string of life that keeps humanity going on endlessly. The woman is tenacious, patient, and enduring.

This quality in a woman has helped her stand with her man, especially those who understand the power of synergy and balance and treat their wives well.

This quality can drive a princess or beauty queen into the hands of a pauper or beast. For most women, it's about how the man makes them feel and what he tells her. This stick-ability can help them bring the gold out of the rock, even if it takes them a lifetime.

For the woman, what is required is to balance emotions with reasoning; what is required is to establish boundaries and understand self-worth, self-value, and the meaning of self-love. You can't give what you don't have. More like the woman described in Proverbs thirty-one, the woman who has self-awareness and understands her worth is indeed a pearl of inestimable value. She must understand that she is valuable, first to God, her creator, then to her world, and, of course, to the man she eventually marries. Anything derailing her from this understanding and mindset should be refuted, rebuffed, and denied a space in her mind.

Every woman was born valuable, like a gold mine; she only requires the right people and the right tools to bring out the best in her; in the same vein, every woman is born vulnerable and may have been crippled by cultures and beliefs, but when you come of age as a woman, when you come to understand your value in Christ, you must put away childishness and refuse to be treated as a victim or weak person. Do not let anybody cripple you in the name of love. True love liberates, nurtures, and builds.

Truly, in their physical makeup, women may be termed weaker vessels; I am convinced the word delicate is also appropriate. But that is where it starts and ends; spiritually, women have been known for strength, tenacity, staying power, and long-suffering. Oh yes! There are boundaries, and every girl must be raised to understand boundaries; no, these boundaries are not fences to keep you in; boundaries are barricades of some sort to keep you safe so that the threat stays out of your space. They are triggers by which you evaluate your emotional terrain beyond the physical.

There are boundaries, and every girl must be raised to understand boundaries; no, these boundaries are not fences to keep you in; boundaries are barricades of some sort to keep you safe so that the threat stays out of your space. They are triggers by which you evaluate your emotional terrain beyond the physical.

You are bound by love to respect others, and courtesy demands that you give honour to whom honour is due. Still, these boundaries also let you know that as a woman, you cannot and should not be taken for granted by the opposite sex just because you are a woman. You are not to be subordinate to any and everybody described as a man just because you are a woman. Please do not label me a feminist. I want every child of God to know that girls, ladies, and women are special. They are special to God, and indeed, there are benefits for all who acknowledge this truth.

The woman is the mirror of nature and God; she must understand grace and be a true reflection of grace in every aspect of her life. In words, in deeds, in mannerisms, in character, in the affairs of life and the affairs of men.

The woman is the mirror of nature and God; she must understand grace and be a true reflection of grace in every aspect of her life. In words, in deeds, in mannerisms, in character, in the affairs of life and the affairs of men.

Somebody said grace is a lady, wisdom is a lady, humility is a lady, and peace is a lady. As a lady, let people find it easy to describe you with these adjectives. Even if you work in the army, be graceful, and even if you turn out to be a janitor, as a woman, still be graceful.

As a lady, when dealing with your spouse, you have to be respectful and courteous. No matter your job description, be soft-spoken and firm at home and anywhere.

It is expected, and it is noble, too. Women do not have to raise their voices to make a point. Do not learn the hard way; practice grace and gracefulness, let your walk be graceful, and let your words be seasoned with grace.

Many things may win a husband's heart; one is gracefulness, a direct outflow of humility and love. Often, humility and love are intertwined. Hardly will you find a graceful person who is not humble and often peaceful and peace-loving.

Even though people are generally shaped by their upbringing, a woman can practice grace and be graceful; God formed her in grace and rest, and she can fit into that vessel when placed in the right environment. Be a woman; be graceful just because you can. No, nobody is trying to put you into some form of stereotype. Be graceful; grace will sponsor you and give you peace that passes all understanding. This is God's perfect model for the woman God made, and that is you.

ACTION NOTE/CHECKLIST

1. Understanding is a key requirement in marriage, and the fine lines must be underscored.

2. A man who hits you before marriage will hit you twice as much when you get married. As long as you tolerated it before saying yes, I do

3. Love doesn't have to hurt so bad, even though we may be required to make some sacrifices in love (enduring domestic violence is not a sacrifice. It is a suicide mission)

4. Nobody has a right by any standard to hit anybody, especially in marriage; we must resort to dialogue at all times and seek mediation where required

5. Love with wisdom and be involved in your marriage. Unwholesome boundaries can breed insecurity.

6. Insecurity can ignite suspicions, over-inquisitiveness, and abuse of all sorts, and that can create a lack of trust friction, which tends to weaken the marriage

7. Be careful of hearsay, gossip, and ungodly counsel against your spouse... if you rock your boat, you will be left alone to drown.

8. Love is a powerful pillar for marriage; though sometimes not enough, it cannot be removed from the equation. God gives endearing love; as you have received it, so give it.

PRAYER

Dear Lord, I humbly ask that You grant me all the graces I require to build a marriage that will become a refuge for me and many others from the storms of life.

In Jesus matchless name -*Amen*

Please write at least three key things concerning your thoughts, resolutions, and actions concerning what you learned.

Thoughts

1.____

2____

3____

Resolutions

1____

2.____

3____

Action to be taken

1____

2____

3____

4

WHY DID YOU MARRY THAT PERSON?

Someone said if the purpose of a thing is not known, abuse is inevitable. How true. By extension, it is not likely that one will ever achieve the purpose of a thing if it is not known to that person. That is a chance you do not want to take, especially in marriage. Marriage is a force that needs a driver; otherwise, it may go wrong. Purpose is what drives marriage in the right direction. Therefore, all the stakeholders must understand why they are getting married first and marrying the person they marry. In essence, beyond knowing the reason for marriage and why you want to get married, you also need to know why you are getting married to that person and why the person is getting married to you.

Love is based on unwritten codes of understanding and tolerance, the terms and conditions on which every love relationship and marriage runs. On the surface, not everybody can marry just anybody; those things that attract one person to a particular person make the idea of love specific and not mass production. Marriage is also specific. Someone may be attracted to you and claim to love you but also say they cannot marry you.

It is okay to feel hurt, but it is important to ask why.

Generally, men are more intentional about what they want in marriage and the woman (wife) that will help them achieve their marital goals. For example, not every man wants to marry an attractive woman, and even if they do, often, there must be something else. A man may have an affair with a pretty woman but never propose to marry her for reasons best known to him. It may sometimes be about more than just the outward appearance of things with the men. But some men will marry a woman because she is beautiful outwardly; that may be why that man sometimes believes she is his trophy and bank statement. He may feel better when he goes out with her and when he is with his family and friends. For that kind of man, you must keep it in check; the weight and looks must all be the correct size even after three or more children. It is that important to him. Anyone who needs help understanding why they got married to the person they got married may just be getting on a train to a place they think should bring happiness but has no road map, timeline, or visuals for the journey.

> **Anyone who needs help understanding why they got married to the person they got married may just be getting on a train to a place they think should bring happiness but has no road map, timeline, or visuals for the journey.**

There are many questions you should ask each other, more like conversations, and these conversations are not stereotypes but very individualistic and personal. When you listen with your head and watch out for body language, you will often hear much more than just listening with your heart and hands.

So if a man marries a woman because he wants four children, for example, to be specific, he wants two sons amongst them, the woman will likely be blamed by her husband for having four daughters, and even if the husband were a clergyman or an atheist, he might seek to have two sons outside the confines of marriage; for him, that does not mean he doesn't love his wife.

Typically, many of the gender-called men think this way, except that particular man has built a close relationship with God and always seeks to align his desires with God's word and perfect will.

Oh! Anybody can pray, fast, and try to persuade God to give him anything, just anything. Even the wife or husband you married may seem like an answered prayer. But, when trouble starts, you begin to wonder where God is. I know I prayed and met the person in the church; where did I miss it? I heard God, and so forth.

Yes! You prayed, but did God say it was His perfect will? Remember, there is the

a. Good Will
b. Acceptable Will
c. Perfect Will of God

You must know for sure why you married the person you married so that when contrary voices start playing in your head in the face of challenges, you will not be flustered and seek a bailout in the form of separation and, eventually, divorce. Just as important as you know why you married the person, your spouse ought to know why you married them and be willing to do what is required to fulfil the purpose. Often, some Christians try to arm-twist God into granting them their desires rather than His desire. Prayer is fellowship with God and two-way communication, but for some, it may be a means of informing God about their heart desires and asking Him to give His blessings without seeking His perfect will in the first place.

There are many references in the Bible where people have practically led the way and expected God to follow them. An example is Mr Lot, Abraham's nephew, who chose the plains of Sodom and Gomorrah, which didn't become God's perfect will. You cannot ask for God's leading; at the same time, you are running ahead of Him and telling Him what to do in your relationship/marriage.

Leadership or commitment in the house of God does not equate to the maturity and understanding required to build a beautiful marriage. That a brother or sister is committed to the things of God and in church does not automatically translate to commitment in a relationship, nor does it mean they have invested in themselves the knowledge and understanding required to deal with the affairs of life as it concerns marriage, even if he or she were a clergyman or woman. Often, how we manage our relationships directly reflects our upbringing, personality type, family background, and social standing.

> **That a brother or sister is committed to the things of God and in church does not automatically translate to commitment in a relationship, nor does it mean they have invested in themselves the knowledge and understanding required to deal with the affairs of life as it concerns marriage, even if he or she were a clergyman or woman. Often, how we manage our relationships directly reflects our upbringing, personality type, family background, and social standing.**

Do not get me wrong, there are many good marriages out there, but there are a lot of bad marriages, too. The Christian couple must take deliberate steps to work out their marriages and make it work, even for one reason: to show a worthy example of the gospel of the Lord Jesus Christ. It is a good enough reason to work out your marriage, and it does not have to cost you your life. It is even more critical and expected that you do so as a leader in the house of God. Yet, one person cannot make a marriage work; you only decide and do what you can in an enabling environment. It may be difficult to work out a marriage where your spouse constantly beats you and threatens to kill you; if you continue, you may be killed one day. Abuse in marriage is not limited to domestic violence. Those married to a Narcissistic spouse may suffer more trauma and injury emotionally and to their mental health.

If many understand the implications of being a spiritual leader, they may be more prayerful and discerning when choosing the one they marry. A man of God said that two choices are most likely to thwart or derail you from your destiny in life if you choose wrongly

1. one is the person you marry
2. and the second one is the career you choose.

For all the reasons we must get married, let it be for the primary goal of helping us fulfil our destiny and calling in life first. Because no matter how much money you have and the capacity to acquire, own, and afford anything, if you do not fulfil your calling, you have lived an empty life.

For all the reasons we must get married, let it be for the primary goal of helping us fulfil our destiny and calling in life first. Because no matter how much money you have and the capacity to acquire, own, and afford anything, if you do not fulfil your calling, you have lived an empty life.

Understand Your Calling First.

How can you choose a life partner when you do not know your calling? You must understand the CALL before entering into any partnership to fulfil it. Remember, marriage is not an end but a means to an end. If we look at it from this perspective, we will be much more mindful and, indeed, be prayerful about whom we marry. The goal is to fulfil your destiny in life. Marriage is supposed to help you achieve that if it is part of your destiny in the first place because the Bible says one will chase a thousand and two ten thousand. Marriage is an example of this synergy when you get it right.

There are beautiful marriages amongst people of other beliefs and religions, and that may be true. Still, for the Christian, you must understand that your life is not ordinary. The day you got born-again and became a Christian, you are bought with a price, not with corruptible elements like silver and gold but with the precious blood of the Lord and Saviour Jesus Christ; you are different and have a calling on your life.

Being a Christian must inform all your decisions, especially who you marry. I have seen Christian ladies and, indeed, Christian men choose to marry for many other reasons, including tribal, professional, and family classes rather than the perfect will of God; that in itself is as much an error as it is an error to marry a brother or sister from church without seeking the perfect will of God.

That somebody is a born-again Christian does not mean it is God's perfect will for you to marry the person. Yet you must marry a born-again Christian if you want to walk in the perfect will of God for you.

The above statement is not to confuse anybody but to emphasise that you have to pray and get the leading of the Holy Spirit to marry that particular person and not just marry any born-again Christian. Yet, it would be best if you married a born-again Christian because you cannot be unequally yoked with an unbeliever. Marriage is the perfect example of yoking, so one must be careful about who you marry.

 The summary is that you must know what your calling in life is, what your profession is, and even as specific as your career path before you choose a life partner; please note I said you must know, not necessarily that you must have arrived. It is a journey and a process to a destination, and you need someone beside you cheering you on, encouraging you, walking the ropes with you, and believing in you as you go along. In this journey to living your calling, there will be obstacles, and sometimes, you may be too discouraged, disappointed, beaten, and hopeless to want to continue. Still, this person called your wife or husband would represent a thousand voices to cheer you on, help you get back on your feet, and give you the support to enable you to breast the tape.

> In this journey to living your calling, there will be obstacles, and sometimes, you may be too discouraged, disappointed, beaten, and hopeless to want to continue. Still, this person called your wife or husband would represent a thousand voices to cheer you on, help you get back on your feet, and give you the support to enable you to breast the tape.

Sometimes, they help you put in a few bricks to support your goals and make your vision come alive. Knowing your calling before marriage is a critical and integral part of a successful and beautiful marriage. Make no mistakes about it; the person who helped and supported you the most becomes your hero and earns your respect, be it your father, mother, sibling, or friend, and those are the people that matter most to you in the evening of your life.

One of the primary reasons for the disconnect between couples later in life is when there are no shared values, such as when the children have all gone off to college. When no memories were made together as husband and wife in the earlier days of your marriage, when the eyes were filled with hope, the feet were strong enough to run and obtain, the heart was young enough to dare, and the fear of failure had not crippled the feet. What will be left to keep you together? There are phases in a man's life, and there are phases in a woman's life.

Middle Age Crisis Could Happen.

Many people marry in the afternoon of their lives. After some years comes middle age with its challenges; in that curve, some encounter mid-life crises which may last from four to twenty years, and it is at this point that all your values will be tested the most, be it faith, faithfulness, patience, long-suffering, endurance, trust, loyalty, love, integrity and many more.

Life is a journey, not a destination; there may be highs and lows. Sometimes, the most significant opportunities in some people's lives come early; they may be sensitive enough to know the time of their visitation, like the sons of Issachar. At this point, you make the best decisions and make good use of those opportunities in your path to make investments that could give a soft landing to secure your future, especially financial investments. But some may not be sensitive to the timings in their life and think that they can do what they want with the opportunity and still have enough time to make it later in life.

Then, suddenly, the realisation that they may have missed a once-in-a-lifetime opportunity dawns on them, and insecurity and regrets kick in. Before long, they blame their spouse for their wrong decisions. Some even blame themselves and are unable to forgive themselves. Dissatisfaction can flow into other areas of their lives, and the most likely person to suffer the consequences of their crisis is their spouse and, by extension, their marriage.

Be intentional about why and whom you marry. For those already married, you can still look into your heart and seek clarity as to why you married the person you married. If, for some reason, the idea or expectation you had is no longer in sight.

Make an effort to rekindle it, and if it seems too obvious it's a lost glory, then stay and let love bind you both together for love's sake.

Will you be firm or frail? Will your love and the profession of your vows stand the test of your faith? Beyond love, will love be enough? You decide. Love is a decision first; after all is said and done, love will remain a decision you make.

Understanding Love Language

As a key part of understanding yourself, you should know your love language and how your spouse may mirror that. This will increase your capacity to connect with your spouse and help you love each other with understanding.

There are five love languages, and they include:

a.   Words of Affirmation.

b.   Quality time

c.   Gifts giving

d.   Acts of service

e.   Physical touch

This classification of Love Language was made popular by Dr Gary Chapman.

Understanding your love language will help you understand your emotional needs, and you can help your spouse connect with you emotionally. Understanding your spouse's love language will help you better understand their emotional need and improve your connection with them.

Love relationship in marriage should be more of a giving relationship and not one that is characterised by demands, which happens a lot of times as many people try to ask for what they think they need from others instead of allowing it to flow from a place of understanding; so we feel drained and describe the other person as being too demanding and insatiable. All these lead to a disconnect in marriage.

Everyone has a primary and a secondary love language. Once we learn to speak it, there will be robust communication, which is essential for any relationship to grow and blossom. Love is an action word, and it should not be passive; every confession of love must be followed by an action correlating to the word love; our physical design up makes room for romantic love, but the human person is not just a physical being, they also have emotional and mental needs and the need and desire to have a connection in the mental and emotional quarters becomes stronger than the physical connection as people grow older.

So when we say we fell in love, it is often on a physical level, which is not enough to sustain a marriage; the mental and emotional become more demanding, and many people's flaws begin to surface. Generally, people complain more about their spouse in areas of their deepest needs. For example, when a spouse complains about their partner being too busy with their work or business, it may indicate that their primary love language is Quality Time.

Often, when people fall in love, the euphoria of the physical attraction does not last forever if not backed by intentional actions that stimulate other areas like their mental, emotional and even spiritual faculties. At the most, the falling-in-love experience built around physical attraction may not last more than two years. That is why some marriages fail. The kind of love that can sustain a marriage is intentional, and it's a decision to work out your differences and uphold your strengths through patience and support for each other.

a. Words of Affirmation: These are positive words of compliments and encouragement to your spouse. They are often not solicited for and come from a place of genuine love and admiration. Genuine compliments like "I love your tie, "or "That dress looks so gorgeous on you", or showing appreciation for something done like "Thank you for picking up the clothes from the laundry" are all words of Affirmation that can encourage your spouse to do more and be at their best at all times.

An important aspect of words of affirmation is the tone of your voice and the fact that the statement comes from a place of genuine love, appreciation and care. Words of affirmation may even be in the form of showing support for your spouse's dream and encouraging them to pursue their goals and aspirations even when they face rejection. Your constant support and validation of their vision and dreams can help them overcome their insecurity in different areas.

Speak with kindness and gentleness, and let them know you have their back even when all else fails. Letting them know you are their biggest cheerleader is an important motivation to help them score high. At any point in your marriage, even when you are making demands beyond your request, a spouse whose love language is words of affirmation listens to your tone, tries to decipher the motivation behind your request and will be willing to go the extra mile to meet your requests if they perceive it to be from a place of respect and love, knowing that you are requesting because you trust them and believe in their capacity to meet your need not because you want to ridicule them or expose their inadequacies. This positive perception can increase closeness and bring more intimacy into your marriage.

When you learn to speak your spouse's love language, especially those whose love language is the word of affirmation, you must compliment them in the presence of friends and family members, even in their absence. This can boost their confidence and resolve to do more. You can also send positive words of affirmation to your spouse via text messages, chats, emails and even as cards or love notes, not only on occasions of their birthdays but as a regular occurrence in your marriage.

b. Quality Time: Spending quality time with your spouse may be more important to them than working extra hours at the office to buy them gifts. For those whose love language is Quality Time, it is not enough to be around; you must spend quality time talking to them face to face, sometimes playing games or watching their favourite television show with them, and holding hands or touching them even for a short period means a lot. Being within physical distance and engaging with them is very important.

For example, a man whose love language is quality time would rather have his wife sit with him and ask him how his day at work went than her doing house chores while he tries to talk to her about how his day went. Even though what she is doing is important, he considers her undivided attention to him at that point not just more important but urgent. Note that quality time does not necessarily refer to the length of time spent together, but the connection created memories shared and emotions elicited by that time spent together.

There are different aspects to quality time; sometimes, people want to have quality conversations around any subject, and even if it is not of interest to you, knowing that it is your spouse's love language you engage in. Sometimes, your spouse may want to share their problems with you not so you can advise them but so you can listen and empathise with them. The key is to know what resonates with the person and genuinely make an effort to give them a soft landing at all times.

Where the person wants quality conversation, you must practice sympathetic listening by being present at the moment and showing your emotions in line with the conversation through your body language and facial expressions more than your verbal response. It is very important to make eye contact with full concentration and nod to show they have your attention and that you feel their pains or joys.

c. Gift Giving: Some people value gifts more than words or your presence; they may see gifts as an expression of love and sacrifice. They feel that the gift is a symbolic representation of your love and appreciation in the sense that though you were absent or not in touch, you were thinking of them, which is why you got them a gift.

The exchange of rings during a wedding ceremony further expresses this belief that the ring is an outward expression of the inner and deeper feelings of those who exchanged that ring gift, a never-ending circle signifying endless love. We must, however, state here that just as our faces differ, our love language differs from person to person. Yes, it is important to give gifts; it is far more important to understand your spouse's love language and learn to speak it.

If this is the primary love language of your spouse, it might help to note the things they may have expressed interest in, want or appreciate at different times and make an effort to get it for them as often as possible or on special occasions. Unfortunately, some people may not care how you treat or talk to them as long as you buy or give them gifts. Interestingly, giving gifts is one of the easiest love languages if you can afford them when your spouse holds them in high esteem.

A total change in your perspective of money is required to be able to fulfil your spouse's desire, especially if you are a person who loves to save money. We must also not undermine that even for those whose love language is gift-giving, being present with them physically is a gift of inestimable value.

d Acts of Service: The fourth love language is acts of service; little acts of kindness and love matter a lot, things like breakfast in bed when they are sick, doing the laundry, bathing the children, shopping and other day-to-day activities that require time, energy, planning and being available are appreciated. Sometimes, people do these things during dating and courtship and later stop doing them after getting married, forgetting that these simple acts may have been the reason the person fell in love with you in the first place. The things that make the person happy before marriage are often very important to the person in marriage.

When it comes to acts of service as a love language, you must put away your understanding of stereotypes concerning traditional roles of men and women in the home when married. Remember, some years ago, women didn't work eight to five-jobs; most of what they did was within the home, but today, a lot of women go to work outside the house; some of them are senior executives in their white-collar jobs and sits in offices where they make decisions that affect their organisation on a global scale, yet they are expected to clean the house, cook the meals, manage the children and do all of these as professional housewives.

If this is the love language of your spouse, especially the ladies, the men must make adjustments and learn to speak their wife's love language as fluently as possible for there to be peace and fulfilment in the marriage. Clarity is important for the relationship to thrive. A woman whose love language is acts of service should not hesitate to ask for help from her husband when in need.

e. Physical Touch: It has been established that children who grow up with a lot of love, hugs, kisses, and physical touch grow up to be adults with healthier emotional dispositions. In marriage, there are no boundaries when it comes to physical touch. However, with people whose love language is physical touch, most would hug, kiss, hold hands, and want bodily contact most of the time. Generally, they seek public displays of affection to validate their love. One can use physical touch to ignite lovemaking and sexual intimacy in marriage.

Another important factor is to note that the desire for physical touch as a love language should not be misinterpreted as a lead that your spouse wants intimacy, especially as a lady; hugging a man can arouse him sexually and give him the wrong signal. Meanwhile, she wants a kiss on the forehead and a touch on the cheeks.

There are different kinds of touches; when your spouse is going through difficult times, hugging them, holding their hands or patting them on the back are examples of non-sexual touches that can be used to comfort them.

In all of these, remember that even if it is not your primary or secondary love language, you learnt to speak, and you are speaking the language because it's a great way to foster connection with your spouse, create memories and improve your marriage is a valuable investment.

Compare learning to speak your spouse's love language to having to learn a foreign language because you have to live in another country where their primary language is different from the language in the country of your birth or origin; you learn to speak that language so you can effectively communicate and relate with the people amongst whom you are now living.

Personality Type

Know your personality type. A lot has to be done in that area, and I recommend you take some personality tests to know yourself better. Be mindful that most of these tests are introspective, which means they are self-evaluating, and you must be sincere to get an accurate analysis.

Work on improving the areas you find you are deficient. Some authors have created some classifications that can help you understand yourself better. The Myers-Briggs personality test has been one of the most popular tools for personality tests. Authors Tim and Beverly LaHaye are also known for these four general personality types

a. Sanguine

b., Choleric

c. Melancholic

d. Phlegmatic

Another critical area to appraise yourself is to outline your values; our values propel us and drive our everyday lives. What are the things that make you look forward to another day? What things turn you on or off in people and around you? Some examples of values include the following:

1 Respect for self and others

2. Responsibility

3. Honesty

4. Integrity

5. Respect for boundaries

6. Perseverance

7. Hard work/dignity of labour

8.   Empathy

9.   Charity

10.   Family bonds or ties

I will encourage you to look into the meaning of these values and find a middle ground where you have shared values and build on them.

ACTION NOTE/CHECKLIST

1. Seek to understand the reason somebody married you and why you married the person, then find the middle ground for peace and harmony and more love.

2. Does the person understand why you are their choice?

3. Never go into Marriage with the intention or hope of changing the person (only God can change a person), so stop trying

4. Whatever you saw before you got married, be prepared to live with it forever; the most you can do is pray about it

5. Marriage is not a one-way ticket to happiness and possibilities; your happiness is first your responsibility, and do what you can to make others happy, but don't kill yourself

6. Bring something to the table; keep bringing something to the table even when it seems like the other person has all it takes.

PRAYER

May God help you to discern what is required of you and grant you the grace to make your home a haven from the storms of life.

In Jesus' Matchless Name-*Amen*

God bless you, and I love you.

Please write at least three key things concerning your thoughts, resolutions, and corresponding actions.

Thoughts

1.____

2____

3____

Resolutions

1____

2.____

3____

Action to be taken

1____

2____

3____

5

MAKING IT WORK (A SHORT STORY)

The hustle in a typical fast-paced city like Lagos, Nigeria, is real. It can pose a challenge to many people, especially couples, who may face the many demands of work, family life, and life itself and the need to balance all of them.

As a couple, Damien and Jannelle have been married for some years and blessed with two lovely children. They must constantly make decisions that will work for them on all fronts. With the understanding that everyone is trying to manufacture a living than make one, the decision to be each other's support system, best friend, biggest fan, and go-to-person is tested through the very fabric of their Marriage.

****

It is another busy day in the city. Jannelle is trying so hard to be on schedule; at least she had an itinerary, and everything seemed to be going well until the boss called for an emergency meeting after lunch; this means she may not be able to make it to the bank as she had planned to do with her lunchtime because she has to stay back to prepare for the meeting...

Jannelle had no option but to reach Damien for help; with what exactly? She can't even figure it out. She wants to prevent any argument about why she picked up the children late from school, why dinner was not ready on time, and so on. So, she puts a call through to her husband.

..." Hello babe, how is your day going?" Jannelle said with tension in her voice. "I'm good, and you? I hope you're good. You're sounding a bit tense," Damien responded.

"Yeah! My boss just called for an emergency meeting after lunchtime, and I need to prepare for the meeting. Please can you help with the shopping and possibly plan to pick up the children? Because the meeting might run late," Jannelle reeled out.

There was silence at the other end..." hello, babe, can you hear me?" Jannelle continued

"I can hear you; I'm just trying to figure out how to work that into my already tight schedule for today," Damien said..."anyway, send me the list, and let me see how much I can take off your plate. I think picking up the children is critical, and that is by five pm, which is already around the corner."

She could not hide the excitement and relief she felt when her husband accepted to help her. "thanks, babe, you are the best, thank you. I need to get off the phone now; I will send you the list and any other details. See you soon"...

It wouldn't be easy for Damien to be called up at such short notice to take on such responsibilities. Still, he is going to see how he can support his wife because that is one decision he has made, to be his wife's go-to-person for any and everything; of course, God is the number one person for them, but when it comes to superheroes, he would be there for her, no matter the cost.

It is easy to conclude that Jannelle may be taking advantage of Damien, but on the flip side, have you considered the implications of having to explain to her husband why the children stayed late at school and the implications of that on both Damien and the children?

You know, it is possible for her husband to feel out of place if he finds out that his wife had asked the neighbour to help her pick up their children and keep them in their house.

The big deal is understanding each other and what resonates with each of you; communication can bring about this much-talked-about understanding. There is no way anyone can understand the things that are important to you if you don't have good communication between you.

Like any regular couple, Damien and Jannelle have their circle of friends and relatives, which means there could be some influencers and stakeholders. Still, they understand that their responsibility is to each other first and always, and their life as a couple and all that happens between them in Marriage is not for public consumption ...

When Jannelle drove into their apartment, she could smell the aroma from the kitchen. Though relieved that she didn't have to start making dinner so late and also help with the homework and household chores, she wondered if the exact bargain was struck to make the food last as long as she had budgeted.

"Hey, babe! Thank you so much; what will I do without you?" My life would have been chaotic without you, my rock and superhero. May God bless you and bless the mother that gave birth to you, and the father that paid your school fees, and ..." Jannelle's voice filled the house with praises for her husband "abeg is enough, come and take over the cooking.

I engaged the children in their room with the Cartoon channel, and let me see if I could give them their bath; they just ate some rice from the eatery, though they wanted pizza. I told them they couldn't have pizza except mummy bought it. Before I forget, they're yet to complete their homework, though we started already..."Damien responded as though he was presenting his report card to his wife.

"What will I do without you?" how can I pay you for making my life so easy?" Janelle asked, grabbing Damien from behind.

"We will settle that in the other room", Damien responded as he dashed out.

They both laughed and went on to complete the tasks at hand.

When Jannelle finished her chores, she called Damien to ask if he needed some fruits; when there was no response, she came out to the living room to find him sleeping on the sofa, obviously tired from all the extra things he had to take on.

She sat on the edge of the sofa where he lay and gently stroked his cheek with the back of her hands; when he wouldn't wake up, she bent over to plant a kiss on his forehead, then his nose and finally his lips...

He slowly opened his eyes and yielded to the softness that pressed against his lips.

"I just thought to rest a little. I didn't know when I fell asleep; what's the time?"

"It is past nine already, almost ten pm", she responded softly as though she didn't want to wake him up...

Damien sat up and ate the fruits lazily, "oh, oh! Babe, why did you add pineapple? You know I don't like eating pineapple at night. After brushing, it leaves your mouth with this aftertaste."

"Sorry, it was what we had left in the house. I had already cut it, and it might be off by tomorrow, and I didn't want it to waste," Jannelle responded in defence.

She took the plate to the kitchen and returned to find him sleeping again. She tried to wake him up, and he responded as though he was in a far country; she just laid on him while on the sofa, and then he woke up, and they both went into the other room...

As natural as it seems with Jannelle and Damien, this is the dream for many people in Marriage; there is no flow in the conversations in many homes amongst married people.

But a life of love and mutual respect is possible if those involved decide to work things out. It is a decision that the husband and his wife must make. A happy home, a life of bliss and simplicity, is only a decision away.

The Bible says, 'How can two work together except they be agreed? There is so much power in agreement; husband and wife must learn to be in and walk in agreement.

In Marriage, sometimes, and indeed often, we must all make sacrifices, if not for anything, for the simple purpose of living in peace.

I have come to understand that even if two people lived next door to each other and knew themselves from childhood, that does not mean you understand the person like a book you read for pleasure or examination purposes.

You still need to make an effort to know and understand your spouse and make adjustments to accommodate their weaknesses and excesses rather than trying to change them. Somehow, change comes when the person decides to change for whatever reasons they may choose to change.

Celebrate their strength and emphasise them over their weaknesses and faults, and be their biggest fan and cheerleader.

The message translation puts it like this.

Marriage is not a place to "stand up for your rights." Marriage is a decision to serve the other, whether in bed or out
-1 Corinthians 7:4 *(Message Translation)*

If we go into Marriage with this mindset, I believe many will be in a better place today in terms of happiness, satisfaction and true feelings of bliss and being loved.

The decision to be happy is an individual one; it's a choice, and while we hope that our spouse will play their part in our happiness, as a couple and as individuals, we cannot hinge our happiness on our spouse; it is not their responsibility.

Suffice it to say that the mindset to have is, since I may not be able to determine the exact thoughts running in their mind at any time, I may not be able to determine their specific response or reaction so that I will make excuses for them.

We are wired differently and respond to pressure differently; the best you can do at any point is to seek to understand your spouse and make the best of your relationship at any given time. Do not worry yourself and lose sleep or become sick by being overprotective or over-concerned, but find a balance between genuine concern and playfulness and make sure you pray for them genuinely.

There are real challenges in marriage, and they can run far and deep, ranging from understanding yourselves, your needs, money, expectations and demands, and children. The list is endless. It is important to discuss it, respect each other's opinions or stances, and then agree on solutions to the different challenges, making a deliberate effort to work on them.

Knowing your spouse disregards your opinion and genuine concerns can be a pain. Even if you feel it is trivial, you may be right, but for your spouse, this matter is right now on their mind, and this is important, so respond to them with some level of concern as though you are in their shoes at that point. Reassure them of your support and confidence that everything will be all right. Your concern can even help them get over it more easily and quickly.

One thing you must not make excuses for, however, is how you are treated in your relationship. You must set that boundary from the beginning and at all times. If anybody, especially your spouse, treats you badly for whatever reason, be firm and insist that you would not want to be treated that way; if they repeat it, give them some space to get over their issues.

ACTION NOTE/CHECKLIST

1. Be grateful; remember to say thank you even when your spouse fulfils their obligations.

2. Be reasonable and don't criticise them overtly, especially in the presence of the children or third-party

3. Love genuinely, don't withdraw your love as a punitive or corrective measure. It is an act of betrayal.

4. Choose dialogue over contention. Somehow, it is better to walk away than physically fight your spouse.

5. Know your boundaries and borderline. Don't get pushed into the waters even if you can swim.

PRAYER

Dear heavenly Father, thank you, for you alone can provide all grace, and I know your grace is sufficient for me for all things, even my Marriage.

In Jesus' matchless name -*Amen*

Please write at least three key things concerning your thoughts, resolutions and corresponding actions to improve communication between you and your spouse.

Thoughts

1.______________________________________

2______________________________________

3______________________________________

Resolutions

1______________________________________

2.______________________________________

3______________________________________

Action to be taken

1______________________________________

2______________________________________

3______________________________________

6

GOD'S WAY TO A BLISSFUL MARRIAGE

... Marriage is sacred, and all stakeholders must buy into this truth for them to enjoy the divine blessings tied to it. It is important that you see marriage as a value and uphold the principles God has put in place to strengthen your marriage.

The Bible says...therefore shall a man leave his father and his mother and cleave to his wife...
(Genesis 2:24-25)

The Christian man or woman who does not acknowledge the sanctity of Marriage is likely to deal lightly with the affairs of their Marriage.

In recognition of the sanctity of Marriage, you must recognise your spouse as God's purchased special possession and accord them the honour due to that person as a child of God, regardless of their social, academic or financial status.

It is easy to judge each other's actions and tend to deal with each other the way they behave, but even in this, our Christian maturity must come into play. It would be best not to deal with your spouse treacherously as with an infidel.

Everyone can forgive, and Marriage is a good place to exercise the power of forgiveness. The purpose and will of God for every Marriage are primarily to exemplify the relationship between our Lord Jesus Christ and the Church- which is His body. The Christian Marriage is like a micro Church of some sort. When you say you are a Christian couple, what are you projecting to your world? Are people seeing Jesus in your everyday dealings with each other?

God's divine purpose for your Marriage is to bring forth godly seeds (children that will continue your Christian legacy and carry the name of our Lord Jesus Christ to the cynical and unbelieving world). God lays claims to your children as Christians and seeks to express Himself through them.

We read in Malachi 2:15.

Malachi 2:15

> *"And did not he make one? Yet had he the residue of the spirit. And wherefore one? That he might seek a godly seed. Therefore, take heed to your spirit, and let none deal treacherously against the wife of his youth."*

Also, the Bible says

> *"Train up a child in the way he should go, and when he is old, he will not depart from it"*
> ***(proverbs 22:6)***

Training a child is beyond taking them to church for the Sunday school teacher to give them some scriptures to memorise. Your lifestyle and how you live every day, your words, communication, body language, and even more importantly, your relationship as a couple is where the real training is, in addition to taking them to church.

It is pathetic to find that human beings are being broken right from the comfort of their homes. The children do not understand what love is because they've hardly seen love, not even amongst their parents or other Christian families for the most part. All the love expressed that most of them have seen is mostly on social media or movies, filled with immoral and ungodly content.

This is one of the critical factors plaguing our society today, a society that lacks commitment and true love. Every profession and acceptance of love has terms and conditions. No one wants to walk an extra mile with anyone without asking what is in it for me.

There is a godly way that can help us have a blissful marriage and be truly happy. Often, this path may be narrow and without many promises, but the end is almost always very certain, happy, filled with joy, contentment, and refreshing.

It requires commitment, and both parties must agree to make their walk with God the focal point of their relationship. Both parties must remember that God instituted marriage from the beginning with the first man and the first woman; he arranged their accommodation, job, and career paths. He made the man first, gave the man his job description and terms of reference before making Eve the woman and handed her over to him so that as the head of the department and boss, he could give her a job and train her for the work. With this, there was not meant to be any form or acts of insubordination, rebellion or usurping of authority. This original plan would lead to a life of bliss, pleasure, and peace.

Do not get me wrong, I'm not in any way promoting chauvinism but insisting that there must be order in the house, there must be clear terms of reference and responsibilities, and it's okay if the wife is in a position to do a bit more financially, that does not remove the fact that the man is the head of the house. This is a serious fact for there to be peace in the home.

Remember, we are better off working with the manual the manufacturer provided to run the program or product effectively.

As I stated before, a man or woman's position in church does not directly equate to his or her maturity in handling the affairs of his or her marriage; we have seen clergymen and women produce disastrous marriages. But it is expected that a person's maturity in the things of God should positively impart and reflect in their marriage.

As I stated before, a man or woman's position in church does not directly equate to his or her maturity in handling the affairs of his or her marriage; we have seen clergymen and women produce disastrous marriages. But it is expected that a person's maturity in the things of God should positively impart and reflect in their marriage.

For this to happen, there must be a decision to work out your marriage and allow God's word to have the final say in your marriage. It starts and ends with both husband and wife agreeing to the supremacy of God's word as far as their marriage is concerned. It must be an understanding and statement of commitment to allow God's word to have the final say in their marriage, not culture, not tribalism, not personal opinion, not family, profession or personal pursuit but God's word.

As simple as this may sound, that is the most important thing required. The question then is, how much of God's word do you know, and how much of God's word have you given the power to control, tame and guide you?

It is nearly impossible to love God genuinely and not love your spouse, even if you think you married the wrong person. When you both choose to walk the path God has chosen for you, it can produce great peace and blessings.

Thank God for social media, the Internet, and all the other social platforms that serve as meeting points for our young people today. But honestly, that may be a distraction when we think about dating, courtship and marriage. Before the advent of the Internet, many marriages were born out of genuine interpersonal relationships, where the couple were neighbours, acquaintances from family friends, or schoolmates at some point.

They never really talked about compatibility based on the flimsy excuses we have today; it was more about family values, mutual respect, long-term friendship and common faith and belief. There was no emphasis on getting sexually involved and spending so much time together privately and publicly to know if you are compatible.

For the most part, a lot of those marriages worked out fine.

Let us be guided by God's word and God's Spirit in all that we do in our marriage; when you come to the understanding that the person is the creation of God, God can grant you the grace to understand your spouse, you will not see some of the challenges as insurmountable.

A good marriage is a decision first, and then it is work, and it is giving of yourself.

Please write at least three key things concerning your thoughts, resolutions and corresponding actions to ensure God's word has pre-eminence in your marriage.

Thoughts

1.______________________________

2______________________________

3______________________________

Resolutions

1______________________________

2.______________________________

3______________________________

Action to be taken

1______________________________

2______________________________

3______________________________

7

BALANCING CULTURE AND FAITH

It is a given that marriage is strongly influenced by culture and traditions, and a lack of understanding of the culture in which you were brought up, and your spouse's culture may cause problems. Even an understanding of the culture in which you live is very important for your peace of mind and long life. Ultimately, God's word should instil in us a culture that is befitting and speaks of the very life of God that beats within our hearts. We must allow God's word to culture us.

The Bible says in Mark 7:13

> *"Thus, you nullify the word of God by the tradition that you have handed down. And you do many things like that."*
> *(NIV Translation)*

I strongly advise that people from different tribes and cultures who get married should take time to understand their spouse's culture and help them understand their own.

Interestingly, we have had very many interracial marriages that are thriving; well, we can say that if all we see on social media is true.

My stand is that almost everything in life is largely based on our decisions; if you decide to work on it and have the support of the stakeholders, it is likely to work. We must go into marriage with an understanding to respect people's culture and beliefs no matter how far apart they may be from yours, especially those of your spouse. It's okay for people to change as individuals, but changing culture and beliefs is different; the critical thing is maintaining the live and live stance until things shift if they have to.

Deep inside, culture and beliefs are norms and traditions which guide the everyday life of the people who hold them dear to their hearts. When you hear someone say, "In my place, it is not done like that", the question is, which place? You cannot dismiss the person with a wave of the hand; you must make every effort to diplomatically negotiate out of it if it contradicts your culture, tradition, beliefs, and faith.

Remember, these cultures, beliefs, traditions and norms are the guiding principles by which a group of people live, which have a stronghold on their minds and outlook on life. They see through the window of their culture and beliefs. It informs and shapes their predominant thoughts and, ultimately, their choices in life. When push comes to shove, that is their primary reflex or response, especially if they were raised in such a culture when they were young.

Suppose they were raised with it and lived in their culture in their minds. Often, regardless of where people live in the physical. Where they live in their minds is more critical. So, when you get married, and I must even counsel, before you get married, do a bit of investigation and findings about the culture and basic beliefs of the people to whom you are about to get married, and find out about 'those things that are most surely believed amongst them. Please find a way to bring it up in conversations and observe the person's reaction and body language. Okay, this book addresses issues in marriage.

You can still do the above, but it will be for you to manage your marriage. And I must warn you that if you are going to change anyone, when it comes to issues of culture and beliefs, they run deep, and sometimes change does not come overnight.

A simple example is that there are some cultures, especially in Africa, where certain tribes hold certain beliefs like pride; the men in certain tribes believe that they should not apologise to their wives verbally. So, there is an issue at hand, and they are wrong. Don't expect them to say the word "I am sorry"; instead, they may do certain things like buy you a gift. This may not always work in marriage, especially for those people whose love language does not exactly respond to gifts. As trivial as this may appear, it has ruined many marriages. There are certain classes of people I have met from this culture who are very unforgiving and vindictive; they expect unflinching support from their spouses even when they are wrong, especially the men, because as far as they are concerned as a wife, you are their property and cannot have a contrary opinion, once you do, you are insubordinate and rebellious and not worthy of their love and though they may have loved you deeply, in a sudden twist, they will not only un-love you but can get to the point of hatred. Such will still love the offspring from that marriage.

I know some other cultures that the kindred spirit they exhibit is akin to cultic ties. For these people, their loyalty is first to their biological family and then to their tribe. Everything else is secondary, so if they marry another tribe, they remain a stranger where their biological family or relatives are. Most will always side with their biological family and tribe against their spouse on any subject. I have often observed a high separation and divorce rate from this tribe. Even when they get married to their relatives or other tribes, especially among the ladies, there is a high rate of separation and divorce because of this.

These are strongholds that can drain you and eventually ruin your marriage. It is better to have a cancelled engagement than a failed marriage.

But if you are already married, it is strongly advised that you look into some of these things and ensure they are not drilling holes in your marriage; rather, give attention to them to ensure you manage them in a mutually beneficial space.

Be Tolerant and Accommodating in Marriage

Sometimes, inter-racial marriages are more enduring and loving than inter-tribal marriages. Because often, both parties already anticipate a difference in culture, tradition and general beliefs, and they make provisions for the differences, whether they be pleasant or shocking, we must be that generous in marriage, especially when dealing with inter-tribal and inter-religious differences. (In the case of inter-religious Marriage, this should not be a consideration for the Christian man or woman; however, if you were married to the person before you truly got born again, it may be applicable. Though some people may be dealing with this, by extension, in cases where they are married to someone from another religion, the person is born again, while some members of their family may still be practising another religion.

It would be best to make provisions for the differences in your beliefs, culture and religion. People's culture and religion give them a belief system by which they are primarily identified. We cannot suddenly pull people out of their culture unless they are willing. Putting barricades and fences to isolate them will not give a lasting and favourable result.

For example, there are cases where the husband will forbid members of his wife's family to come to their home and may not even allow children born into that marriage to interact with the wife's tribe and culture. We have also seen cases where women can be so high-handed that they even forbid their husbands' families from coming to their matrimonial homes. This is barbaric and very unfair; how would you pick a single person from their family and whisk them away to Neverland, marry the person, and seek to isolate the person from their relatives, culture and even tribe?

It's so not right. You must be feeling like a super-human who went to hell on a rescue mission; no matter how heroic that may have felt, it's so wrong and may be depressing for the persons and families involved.

> Marriage brings people from different cultures and races together; marriage is supposed to result from love between two people and all that concerns them: their values, friends, families, and much more.

Marriage brings people from different cultures and races together; marriage is supposed to result from love between two people and all that concerns them: their values, friends, families, and much more.

In the Bible, God specifically told the people of Israel not to marry the people of the land they were to occupy because marriage is a very powerful force. Marriage is a unifying force for many. As much as King Solomon loved God, he was lured away from God by his love for strange women. Though a king, when he married these strange women, many of them princesses from other nations, he was compelled to build temples for their gods and ended up worshipping those gods.

It is better not to marry a person from a particular culture than to marry the person and isolate the person from their family, friends and culture. Of course, they may need to make changes and isolate themselves from whatever they may not find right in their culture, but that is left for them. Do not force them to do it; pray for them, and with your love and understanding, they will learn to separate themselves without feeling robbed. This, too, is a form of love, and it is called tolerance.

The impact of culture, beliefs and upbringing on people's lives is far-reaching. For the most part, even if you carry them across several oceans, these must have created in them a value system that ends up dictating the rhythm of their lives to which they dance; no, it's not exactly the house, the cars and those things that are acquired in a faraway country.

People hold fast to their culture and beliefs as a source of living; even their food reflects it. This is one reason we must consider all of these in marriage: love is the first step, and there are several other things between love, and the end must still be love.

This is reflected in people from different parts of the world.

Shared values are critical for a successful Marriage.

In several of the meetings where I am invited to speak with young people looking to get married and married people looking to strengthen their marriages, when asked the question, what is the most important thing you would advise people to look out for in a person to have a good marriage.? I spell the word VALUES in block letters. Shared values are a critical part of any relationship. Values encapsulate how you perceive yourself, how you see the world, how you see and relate with people and how you live your life in general.

Let me explain an aspect of value with the following. As a student at the university, I had a suitor whom I thought I could marry and live happily ever after. We were both students at the university where I attended. One day, we discussed marriage and values, and he said, "If Jesus tarries, is it the same woman I married when I was thirty years old that will remain my only wife when I am eighty?" He went on to explain that it would be boring and colourless, that it would be like eating only one type of meal every day of your life, insisting that one needs variety to enjoy marriage and that variety is the spice of life.

I didn't argue with or disagree with him; I understood where he came from perfectly. That, in a nutshell, is the justification behind polygamy in many cases from the part of the world where I come from.

That, for me, is a value and a strong value for him; it means even if he didn't marry another woman, having a concubine would be an integral part of his married life, except, of course, he decides to renew his mind with the word of God.

As a young woman, that is a red flag, and on that note, I ended the relationship. The truth is, I never discussed the details with him nor our leaders in the Christian fellowship we both attended. It was too significant for me to consider a conviction or further explanation. At all costs, we must evaluate the values we hold dear and those of our spouse and how that impacts our conversations and everyday life.

> At all costs, we must evaluate the values we hold dear and those of our spouse and how that impacts our conversations and everyday life.

Another critical area of values to consider is that, at the end of it all, that may be all you take when all is said and done. For example, someone who believes the end justifies the means may, by extension, think it is okay to defraud someone else to meet their own needs based on the justification that it is a life where there are predators and prey, and survival is the bottom line.

What happened to integrity? Self-respect? Empathy? Humanity? Love and charity? These do not exist in the world of so many people in our society today. Change begins with me, a value I hold dear, and has become one of my mantras is 'Live and let live'. Sometimes, we may have been victims of other people's bad choices, which should not make us bad in ourselves. We do not pay evil forward. Life is not fair sometimes, yet life is fair altogether. Whatsoever a man sows, he shall also reap. Karma is one of the ways life plays fair.

For the one who is married, it is not so easy to try to change someone; what is easiest for you is to manage the person and always extol the good above the bad.

What I would ask the married folks to do is to focus on the things that attracted them to the person in the first place; God help you to focus on the right things, especially if the initial attraction was based on mundane things like money, cars, a good job, even looks do change with time. Your focus must be deep-seated on character, values, and virtues; many other things can be added with learnings, skills acquisition, training, and opportunities. Seek to befriend your spouse, and be empathic when dealing with them, especially their weaknesses. Be kind to your spouse and their relatives. We all need a support system, and it is better not to start a fight where blood ties.

Love your in-laws as much as you love your spouse, and respect your parents-in-law as much as your parents. This is even more important when children are involved- children take a lot with them, much more than you will ever know.

As parents, always consider your parents and the older generation and how their choices and how they lived their lives have impacted your life. Then, think about your choices and decisions and how they will affect your children and others around you. Do not be like Hezekiah, who was content with God's judgement as long as it wasn't going to happen in his lifetime, but it was the bad choice he made that would bring calamity to his children. This is the height of selfishness.

Another aspect of values is that they allow certain practices amongst those who hold such values; a man or woman may seek to marry someone from their own culture or belief system with the mindset that they hold those values highly, too. This incident readily comes to mind.

While at the university, I had a friend who was so passionate about her religion and was dating a guy who was just as passionate; when we were about to leave the university, they got married and seemingly had a good marriage. Time passed quickly, and we all went into the big wide world seeking greener pastures.

Over time, I ran into the lady and we got talking, after we exchanged pleasantries, I asked her about her husband, she told me they were divorced and I was shocked she said the husband insisted on getting another wife and she was not ready to accommodate a running mate sharing her husband with her. I wondered why because that practice was entrenched in that belief system or religion, and I didn't think anyone passionate about that belief system would want to object to polygamy, even though not everybody who practices that religion is a polygamist.

I have also observed the marriages of some people of a particular sect in Christianity; these marriages transcend cultural divides based on their common faith and belief system. Once they marry, they hardly show any dividing line, and even if they do not speak the same language in terms of dialect, their common faith is their strongest binding force. It has proven strong enough to pull them to the centre where everything holds firmly together. These are classic examples of how culture and beliefs form people's values and can affect their lives and marriages, and after all, is said and done, our choices will determine to a large extent what terms we must live our lives on.

The Christian Beliefs in Marriage.

Christians also have a way of life that must guide their interpersonal and marital relationship. When you read through the Holy Bible, you find that a lot was written about marriage even though most of the stories you read are deeply rooted in culture and beliefs; for example, Sarah gave her made to her husband to help her bear children since she was barren, we see Rachel and Leah do the same for different reasons. The New Testament has a different approach to some of these things and speaks explicitly about how husband and wife should relate (read Ephesians 5:22-33) Amplified Classic Translation. Every Christian couple must resolve to allow God's word to run their lives.

This resolution must be binding on all stakeholders and requires intentional living to bring it to pass in the individual life of the one who prefers to be a Christian. The fact that one demonstrates faith and maturity in the house of God and has attained a leadership position does not automatically translate to the maturity required in that person's character in handling their relationship, even in marriage, though it is expected. I must have said this for the umpteenth time in this book. A man or woman's disposition in marriage is directly influenced by their upbringing, personality type and the investment they have made in their personality, especially in deliberately aligning their life with the teachings of God's word.

Remember, there may be other stakeholders who may not be at your level in Christianity, and they have important roles to play in your marriage; for example- parents or parents-in-law, as the case may be.

Christian maturity requires that you exhibit patience, empathy, understanding, and love to see that your marriage works.

The issue of culture and tradition is another good reason why a Christian must marry a Christian and, where possible, Christians of the same sect because sometimes even love is tribalistic.

> **Christian maturity requires that you exhibit patience, empathy, understanding, and love to see that your marriage works.**

> **When you become a Christian, who holds the word of God as contained in the Bible as truth? You take on the instructions in the Bible and apply them to your Marriage without giving it a different interpretation. God's word is God's intervention in any situation, and the word of God supersedes all cultures and traditions. This may be difficult to accept, but it is the truth.**

When you become a Christian, who holds the word of God as contained in the Bible as truth? You take on the instructions in the Bible and apply them to your Marriage without giving it a different interpretation. God's word is God's intervention in any situation, and the word of God supersedes all cultures and traditions. This may be difficult to accept, but it is the truth.

While having high expectations in marriage is okay, it is highly recommended that everyone goes into marriage with the required skill set to manage their expectations. Some marriages break because of failed expectations, and we must know and understand that sometimes love is not enough to keep a marriage. We can tell someone I love you. But you know I love you; what will I do without you? Someone can say and be told this over and over again, and twenty years later, still walk away and continue to say I love you, but I can not live with you.

Where culture and beliefs come in, the roots run deep. They may have branches, so despite all the love they may have for each other if they cannot manage their cultural differences, you will find that love indeed may not be enough to sustain a marriage; the earlier we understand this, the better and safer and more likely we may be able to hold our marriages together.

On that note, if culture and belief have been a challenge in your marriage, you must have some serious conversation about it, especially if it affects your faith and then agree to some dos and don'ts. This should be done in the best interest of making your marriage work and not as an excuse to end your marriage.

ACTION NOTE/CHECKLIST

1. Marriage involves other people in your world, so it is important to consider the big picture.

2. Make room for your in-laws in your heart and your home.

3. Do not seek to change people to fit your narrative; sometimes, our strength is in our diversity.

4. Never nurse a feeling of insecurity when your spouse is with their tribe and speaks the language- a kindred spirit is not often a negative spirit.

5. Do not weaponise your culture and use it as a tool to control and manipulate your spouse- this, too, is a form of witchcraft.

6. Be guided by God's word, and when culture seeks to divide or humiliate your spouse, insist on God's word before your family or tribe.

7. Ultimately, you are Christians, and the Bible says if any man is in Christ, he is a new creature; old things are passed away. Never forget that.

PRAYER

May God the Father, Son, Holy Spirit, and the word of God always take the pre-eminence in your life and your marriage.

In Jesus' Matchless Name-*Amen*

Please write at least three key things as they concern your thoughts, resolutions and corresponding actions to ensure God's word has pre-eminence in your marriage above the culture and beliefs that seek to divide you.

Thoughts

1.____

2____

3____

Resolutions

1____

2.____

3____

Action to be taken

1____

2____

3____

8

FINANCIAL OBLIGATIONS IN MARRIAGE

Marriage has obligations and responsibilities; husband and wife must understand their obligations to make the best of their union. Sometimes, problems arise when a husband or wife cannot identify, acknowledge, accept, and fulfil their obligations in marriage.

The Christian husband must take care of his family; that family begins with his wife and often ends with his wife in old age. The Bible says a man who does not provide for his family has denied the faith and is worse than an infidel- (1 Timothy 5:8); it is that serious. It is recommended and necessary for a woman to have and bring something to the table, but the husband must work hard enough to provide for the family, not banking on what the wife has.

As a wife, you must support your husband, and that may include financial support. No matter what a woman earns, she must be willing to submit to her husband at the level where he is and support him, not insisting on him doing everything to accommodate her wants, especially if he doesn't have it yet.

This does not, however, erode the fact that the husband must provide for his household, including his wife.

Any man who decides that because his wife earns more and therefore must provide for the house, he will automatically short-circuit the grace God has given him to head his family financially, which may reflect in other areas of his life sooner or later.

Providing for your wife beyond the household necessities is a way of expressing your love, which is in accordance with God's word and comes with its dividends. The man is the head of the house, and this headship comes with obligations, responsibilities, and blessings. I make this statement, particularly to those of the Christian faith.

The Wife and Her Money.

It is essential to clarify that the above postulation does not suggest that the wife does not have responsibilities regarding financial obligations in marriage. I must stress that obligations and responsibilities are different, and the difference is required to drive this point home.

It is the husband's obligation, that is, it is his legal and moral duty primarily to provide for his family. But the wife must also know she is responsible for financially supporting her husband if needed. It is expected of her to do so. This may be necessary to allow him to make some capital investments they will enjoy in the evening of their lives. Such investments could include investing in real estate to ensure they have a roof over their head and something to fall back on when they can no longer work so hard on a day-to-day basis. Everything is straightforward about the above.

When a woman marries, she takes on her husband's name and becomes one flesh with him. She is an integral part of her husband as one entity, as we see in the Bible, for what God has joined together, let no man put asunder. However, referring to her income as her money for accountability is vital. Where there is a shared vision, transparency, understanding, and love, money should be a mutual thing in marriage in times of small beginnings and when it is in abundance. However, money has been one of the biggest challenges in marriage, whether too little or too much.

Money is an amplifier, and if anyone possessing money has not built character or does not understand boundaries, money can throw the person off focus, whether too little or too much money. This is one of the reasons some people change after marriage, especially those with a rags-to-riches story. Here is a couple who held on to each other from their humble beginning and then worked very hard together to accomplish their dreams of riches and prosperity, and then boom! The money comes, and the man becomes another man.

So a woman sticks with you for five, ten, or more years, patiently waiting and managing with you, praying for you to hold it all together, hoping and sometimes believing in you more than your own biological family does, that one day you will make it and become the rich, prince charming to give her a beautiful happily ever after life in the evening of her life.

But you think, now that you have money, you can substitute her for other much younger women because, after all, what has she contributed apart from making babies? Really! Know this: staying married to a man through hard times, especially when making babies, is one of the most challenging jobs in this world as a woman; know this and know peace.

Sometimes, in this condition, there is a lot to cover up; she drops her pride and goes the extra mile to fill in the blank spaces for you, reaching out to family, friends, and sometimes foes, and praying and hoping you never find out where that loaf of bread came from. It is hard work, and if you find a woman who did that, please treat her like a queen because she is the real queen.

Money Management

Wherever you may find yourself, as a woman, a wife, or a single lady, you should engage in decent, gainful business or profession to ensure you have your own money that you can use to support yourself, your husband and children, your family, and your friends. Yes! A woman may require financial support to take care of herself; women sometimes have their obsession, and you can't put that on your husband's plate. That may be wasteful spending. If he can afford it and chooses to gift you things you like, it's okay, but it must not put him under any pressure. What is the value of buying a wig for five hundred US Dollars? Is it an investment? And then you insist on updating your collection frequently? If that is your fantasy, it might be okay for a while, but if you go shopping every three months with five thousand US Dollars for shoes, clothes, bags, wigs, and everything else. And you want to put that bill on your husband's plate when he is not able to afford it through genuine work or business; something is not exactly sitting right with my perception of you, especially If you are a middle-class family in many parts of the world today, you live in a rented apartment and have not started saving for college funds for the children.

If you are a celebrity, that is your game; by all means, please enjoy your money as long as you work for it. But I'm just thinking, as a woman, what if you were patient enough to invest your first five thousand US dollars or more in real estate, even if it was on a piece of land or in land banking for a few months? It might just put you in a space where you can play in surplus instead of never enough, whether as a single woman or married woman.

Men have to manage their money wisely, too. If you spend money fanning your social life every time you get your pay cheque, you are investing in the wind and will reap the emptiness shortly. There will always be friends who will join you in wasting your money if you let them, and there will always be lazy and genuinely needy people who plan with your money regularly. Some of them are meeting all their obligations from regular collections from other people.

I advise working something out for your dependents to enable them to support themselves in the future. As the saying goes, 'Instead of giving a man fish daily, teach him to fish. By so doing, you feed him for life.

Be accountable and responsible for the choices you make when it comes to money. It might be one of the best decisions you would have taken in the long run. Be generous, kind, and helpful, and still be accountable.

Prudence and Savings.

The question of prudence in finances goes for everyone, man or woman, husband or wife. Even if you were born with an inheritance that even inflation or recession cannot deplete, and you think you are in a place where you are sure nothing in this world can affect your prosperity. I insist that as long as it comes to the world's financial system, there is a degree of uncertainty hovering over finances and their long-term value. This in itself may be man-made. By design, the rich in every society constantly try to ensure a gap between the rich, the middle class, and the poor. This has gone on for centuries, and it is not about to stop. Still, you must be prudent and accountable. While we hope for better days in business, on the job, and whatever we do, know that the money you have received is what is vitally yours, so be prudent and develop a culture of saving.

While we hope for better days in business, on the job, and whatever we do, know that the money you have received is what is vitally yours, so be prudent and develop a culture of saving.

Often, many people work and receive money to pay others, but they never really earn any money. They pay the bills, buy food and end up in minus, month in, month out and the years roll by, and they begin to hope to receive a pension that will change their lives forever.

I recommend you take this route: on your income, give God his portion, which is usually ten per cent, then pay yourself a minimum of twenty per cent and have savings of an average of ten per cent.

Then, share the rest amongst your creditors. When your savings have grown, take fifty per cent and invest it.

 If you earn a thousand US dollars per month and live in a house that costs four hundred US dollars a month, there is already a problem: you might need to downsize or increase your income. I have learned by experience and observation that needs will always be there, wants will always be there, and bills will always be there, so it is your prerogative to manage them now so your future may be softer.

You have to save for college funds for the children and the evening of your life (retirement) for a future that may not be so certain in a world of deceit and wickedness; the least you can do is save, Try and save up to three times the cost of your monthly expenses in an emergency account. That means it has to be accessible to you at any time. Wherever you are, start with what you have and make sure you save some money.

One thing is certain: You may never lose money by saving money. Please put it in the right place. Save for investments and be guided when making investment choices. Please do your due diligence; I distrust Ponzi schemes; it's all a scam and shambles. Where is the process? It's a case of robbing Peter to pay Paul. That, my dear, is not an investment. Yes! People may talk about stocks. Please study the market and country's condition and how policies affect investments and stocks. In my opinion, one of the biggest investments with nearly a ninety-five per cent guarantee in return on investments is still real estate. You do not have to play in the big league to get meaningful returns. Please, I come in peace. You know what is most viable in your space. By all means, latch onto it.

There is a lot a family can save for, ranging from capital projects like housing to college funds for the children. This should start, if possible before the children are born, and it should be handled with all the seriousness it requires. The pressure that comes with everyday living when such projects are not planned sometimes leads to anxiety that can lead to high blood pressure and other complications.

I believe issues concerning finances, though challenging, can be handled successfully in some marriages if the husband and wife work together to identify the important and urgent things and decide how to solve them.

If most of the issues in your marriage are issues concerning finance, they can be dealt with as a couple if both parties decide how to go about it and work at it. One person may make more money based on their current placement, work, or business. The first step is to know that you both have become one and that you are making more money down, not make you superior to your spouse and should not make you subjugate your spouse to ill-treatment and disrespect. Have mutual respect.

Yet money problems can seem insurmountable in marriage, so one of the ways to solve it is to identify the things you both must contribute to, and each must meet their obligations.

With some understanding, it may not be necessary to escalate financial issues by bringing a third party to help you decide how to manage your finances. This is different from engaging or seeking the help of a financial or investment professional for advisory reasons. However, escalate it when it becomes a challenge and affects your health. When doing so, there may not be any need to spill the whole thing to the person you are sharing it with, except if it is necessary. For example, you can use percentages instead of amounts to explain the figures.

The focus is on how money management impacts your mental health and marriage. Do not suffer in silence; take as much as you can, and let your spouse know when you are at the edge and request you both see a third party for counselling.

NOTE/CHECKLIST

1. No matter how bad things may be, as a man, you must get up and go fishing because you have a family to care for.

2. Except in cases of ill health, a man has no excuse to be broke; it is akin to bad planning and irresponsibility.

3. Make the right investment in your personality to keep you relevant in your world and space.

4. If you are in paid employment, ensure to make some investment (real estate is highly recommended, not a Ponzi scheme)

5. Plan for a financially stable life outside your career (you can invest in entrepreneurship or trading) while working a nine-to-six job.

6. Every wife must be engaged in a decent job or business; no matter how financially robust a man may be, he may need some help later if the tides change. There is also dignity in labour.

7. It may be necessary to open a joint savings account strictly for the family, and both parties must agree on how the money is spent

8. Starting a college fund for the children before they get to age five is a good way of preparing for the evening of your lives.

9. No matter how certain your projections are, it is the money available to you that you have- make good use of it.

10. Life happens, and tomorrow will always come with blessings and challenges.

PRAYER

Dear heavenly Father, I thank you for the gift of life, Lord; help us to number our days so that we may apply our hearts to wisdom, even financially.

In Jesus' Matchless Name-*Amen*

Please write at least three key things concerning your thoughts, resolutions, and corresponding actions to move your finances forward.

Thoughts

1._______________________________________

2._______________________________________

3._______________________________________

Resolutions

1._______________________________________

2._______________________________________

3._______________________________________

Action to be taken

1._______________________________________

2._______________________________________

3._______________________________________

9

SOME GOOD INTENTIONS (A SHORT STORY)

The relationship between Jannelle and Damien has been a bit tense, and we hope they can resolve all the issues between them as soon as possible.

****

"Thank you, Mr. Luther, for your kind attention. I will send you the documents and details after the land is surveyed next week. In the meantime, I will read through the agreement you drafted." Jannelle said as she stood up to leave.

"The pleasure is mine, madam. Thank you for your valued patronage, " responded Mr. Luther

Jannelle got into her car and drove off; the music from the stereo was loud but not loud enough to drown the voices in her head. She felt it was odd to have seen the lawyer alone, without her husband.

But another voice tells her it is okay; a woman should have her investment as a backup, so if anything happens to her husband, it will be a pleasant surprise to fall back on her investment.

Besides, telling him she has such money may make him want to become lazy and not work so hard anymore. The voices in her head compete to gain dominance.

Jannelle jolted back to reality from the ringtone coming from her phone. She glanced at the phone, and it was Damien; she was going to take the phone call but chose not to, wondering how she would tell him where she was coming from since she hadn't told Damien she would see the lawyer. The phone rang out and rang again and again.

It was a long day for Damien, and he thought since he couldn't speak with his wife, he would stop by her office and let them drive to a cool spot and relax over drinks and food.

The presence of his mother-in-law has given them a bit of a break with the children; besides, he thought to get Mama some suya or shawarma to appreciate her.

Damien pulls into his wife's office car park and picks up his phone to call her. Only to see her driving right around the corner. She looked petrified.

"Babe! I've been calling your phone, but there was no response. I didn't know you were driving. Where did you go? Damien asked, leaning over his wife's car window.

"My dear, I just drove out to get some stuff, but I couldn't get there as the traffic was too bad, so I had to turn back. I will try and get them from the grocery store on the way home," Jannelle fumbled as she spoke.

"Okay! I stopped by so we could sneak out to that restaurant, get some food, and relax until the traffic subsided since Mama was around to manage the children. What do you think? Damien said, looking at her.

"That would have been fine; it's just that I'm really tired and would love to get home as soon as possible to help Mama with the children. Can we buy it and take it along instead?

"But we are driving different cars; how do we bond?

"No vex abeg! I will make it up to you; I'm too tired to chill outside the house and then drive again. So I don't sleep while driving. She pleaded with him...

* *

In the morning, as they got ready for work, it was common practice for Damien to check both cars to ensure that the oil, water, and fuel levels were good before letting his wife drive the car. Damien would only allow Jannelle to drive the car he deemed in the best state and take the one that needed attention.

Janelle had kept her handbag in the car…her phone began to ring, and she took out the phone and, seeing the caller, put it off immediately. That startled Damien, who became curious and asked who was calling, and Jannelle replied it was unimportant…

She would later return the call and tell the lawyer to send her messages instead of calling her, especially when she might be home early in the morning or late evening.

Damien was disturbed by his wife's sudden change; he thought it was strange that she would not tell him who was calling her and not take her calls in his presence. He became more observant of her attitude and thought something was wrong…

Later in the day, still worried about his wife's attitude, Damien sent a message to Jannelle requesting that they hang out after work. Meanwhile, the lawyer had requested for Jannelle to stop by his office to sign some documents, or he would send them to her, but she had declined his sending the documents and opted to stop by his office.

Upon seeing the message from Damien, Jannelle ignored it, planning to reply later and inform Damien that she would be working late…

Distracted by the amount of work she had to finish before the close of work, Jannelle forgot to reply to Damien and was reminded by Damien's call. She snapped!

"Hello! Babe, please let me focus at work; let's keep this hang-out for the weekend; it's not even anything special, or am I forgetting something? It's not our wedding anniversary nor birthday, chill, abeg," Jannelle reeled almost in one sharp breath.

Damien was startled; this led to a long pause from his end of the line.

"Hello! Hello! Babe, can you hear me? Jannelle queried.

"I can hear you. Are you okay?"

"Hmmm..yeah, I mean not really, so much work; as a matter of fact, my boss just called for a meeting, which is already putting me under pressure as I don't know when we will be done. You can go home. I will be fine."

"It's okay, take care. I will talk to you later," said Damien.

As he drove home, he kept wondering what the matter was; he decided to turn the car around and go to his wife's office area to wait for her. Thinking she is already tense, let me drive behind her when she leaves since she might be leaving late.

Damien was surprised to see his wife leave the office almost immediately after they spoke. "Where is she going? Why is she lying to me? What is happening to my Jannelle?

So many thoughts and questions are running through his mind at this point.

He decided to trail her….

Once he knew, she went to the lawyer's office. He was pained and felt a tight knot in his stomach. Myriads of thoughts ran through his mind in a flash…" It's a lie, it can't be happening, Luther? No! Jannelle is seeing Luther?" his thoughts were louder than all the buzzing from the honk of the cars on the street.

He took the next turn and made it home, switching between rage and sanity. One thing was sure: he would get to the bottom of this.

When Jannelle got home that night, Damien forced a smile and avoided her as much as he could. When she set the table and asked him to come over for dinner, he declined and said he was not hungry. Jannelle didn't think much of it and went on to eat her meal.

Damien stayed late in the living room, switching from one channel to the other, looking for nothing in particular until he dosed off on the sofa…

"My in-law, my in-law, go and sleep inside your bedroom, please, so your back will not pain you; this chair is too small for you," his mother-in-law said.

But there was no response from Damien.

When Jannelle woke up to find out that Damien was not in bed, she assumed he had woken up earlier, as he often did, to do some work on his laptop at the dining table since she discourages him from working in the bedroom because he often turned on the lights and that usually disturbs her sleep.

****

It has been one month, and Jannelle and Damien haven't been as close as they used to be. Sometimes, Damien would nibble on his food and get up from the dining table as soon as possible. He was avoiding any conversations with his wife. He didn't want to confront her because he knew she was seeing the lawyer. He was waiting for her to come up with an explanation for seeing the lawyer privately and even lying about it.

With all the documents of the land signed. Jannelle was relieved and in a lighter mood. She was willing to play and even hang out with her husband. She didn't think much of the change in his attitude. As far as Jannelle was concerned, he was sulking because she turned down his request for them to hang out.

So, she planned a surprise weekend away since her mom would be leaving the following week. She thought to have this before returning to their usual routine with the children. Jannelle booked a room in a hotel for a romantic weekend getaway with her husband.

"Babe, please, I'm not up to it this morning; I can't drive to work and drive back. Please let me ride with you to your office and take a taxi from there to my office, and then you pick me up so we can ride back together," Jannelle said to Damien.

He was surprised to hear that and said, "I think you should just drive because you don't know if you might have an emergency meeting or something. I may be working late to finish some reports since it's Friday."

"Exactly my point; it's Friday, so we can hang out or stay late. I could come to your office with a taxi if you're working late and wait for you," she said, trying to make eye contact with her husband, who was avoiding her.

Jannelle had packed some of Damien's clothes when they were leaving home. She had sneaked a bag out of the house and put it in the car's trunk without Damien noticing. She insisted on driving when she got to her husband's office at the close of work because she had planned to drive to the hotel she already booked for the weekend for two.

Damien did not resist; he was open to anything now; he thought she had finally decided to tell him whatever she wanted. He expected the worst. The truth is, he had been considering an extra-marital affair that had been in his face in the office for years now. He had even asked the lady out on a lunch date.

He was seeking validation, wondering where he missed it, that his wife would do this to him.

Candlelight dinner for two, Damien's best meals, drinks, and dessert served. None of those moved him. He was uptight and waiting for Jannelle to tell him why she brought him out that night.

Jannelle was being so romantic. She took the bag from the car and requested the key to the hotel room. After taking a shower, she wore the beautiful, sexy lingerie that Damien had bought for her on their third wedding anniversary. Damien was still sitting on the room chair, as tense as ever. These kinds of nights were not new to their marriage. Before now, Damien had looked forward to it, but it was always Jannelle who took the initiative to arrange their getaway.

She sat on his lap and caressed him, "Babe, go and have your bath. Are you so tired? Okay, go to the bathroom and let me bathe you," Jannelle whispered in his ears.

"Why did you do it?"

"Do what?" she responded, pulling away from him.

" Why have you been lying to me?" Damien asked, looking into her eyes for the first time in a while

"Babe, I don't understand; what's the matter? Lie to you about what?

"If you are not ready to tell me the truth, then I will have to leave; I'm not even feeling safe with you anymore."

" Ah, ah! Babe, what kind of talk is this? What happened? I know you were not happy I turned down two date requests. It was all because of work, and I'm sorry, I was tense at work, so I want to make it up to you this weekend. I'm sorry."

Damien reluctantly went to have his bath and lay in bed. Jannelle practically made every move to make the night fun, but the reality is that she was not feeling her husband tonight and wondered why he was so unhappy and implacable. She felt something was wrong but wasn't ready to spoil the mood and thought it would go away naturally…

The thought of Jannelle seeing Mr Luther could not leave Damien's mind, which had discoloured his once colourful and beautiful relationship with his wife.

. . . .

As far as Jannelle was concerned, her intentions were good. It would be a pleasant surprise to finally let her husband know that she had bought land or, even better, built a house when the time comes.

Lessons from The Story

Often, our intentions are right, but our approach or actions may be wrong and this may jeopardise a hitherto beautiful relationship in marriage. Such acts may surprise women, but most men are vexed by them, especially men from some parts of Africa. A woman who goes ahead to buy a property or land and build a house without her husband's knowledge may be perceived as a traitor and dangerous person threatening the security of her marriage.

> **A woman who goes ahead to buy a property or land and build a house without her husband's knowledge may be perceived as a traitor and dangerous person threatening the security of her marriage.**

The least you can do is tell your husband you want to buy land and bring him into the picture. Jannelle should have gone to see the lawyer with her husband and allowed him to go through the transaction with her.

Better still, she should have carried him along when she began negotiating for the land and asked for his input. All the pains and misunderstandings coming from this intended surprise would be unnecessary, and the consequences of the ripple effect would be far-reaching. Trust is a big issue in marriage and all relationships; once broken, it may never be restored to its former state, no matter how much we try to mend the broken pieces, even if we find ways to glow them together and seemingly have a single piece. The lines remain, showing that there has been a crack before.

> Trust is a big issue in marriage and all relationships; once broken, it may never be restored to its former state, no matter how much we try to mend the broken pieces, even if we find ways to glow them together and seemingly have a single piece. The lines remain, showing that there has been a crack before.

These lines are the memories that remind us of the bad times we had when our trust was broken.

Damien should have just come out to let Jannelle know that he had seen her go to the lawyer and demanded an explanation immediately. But your guess is as good as mine: he didn't want to be accused of suspecting his wife, yet he didn't want to believe what he saw was a total misunderstanding. He needed proof, more proof. Proof that he will never get.

Often, we judge others by their actions and judge ourselves by our intentions. It is, however, advisable to give your spouse the benefit of the doubt and ask for clarification instead of building on false assumptions based on the facts you have. They say seeing is believing, but what you may believe because of what you saw may be wrong. Keep the communication lines open and make excuses for your spouse.

ACTION NOTE/CHECKLIST

1 Never take advantage of your spouse's weakness or strength for selfish gains.

2. Don't give in to the temptation of exploiting your spouse because they choose peace over war.

3. Marriage is for the benefit of two working together. Ensure that you put up a unified front at all times. This will multiply your strength.

4. Respect your spouse. Sometimes, there may be disagreement, but that should not make you belittle your spouse.

5 Play by God's rules. It pays to obey the boss. Never take it upon yourself to serve vengeance. Be forgiving. God said vengeance belongs to Him.

PRAYER

Dear heavenly Father, thank you for our trust in you. You cannot be put to shame, and my trust is in you even now to help me do what is good and acceptable in your sight as it concerns my marriage.

In Jesus' matchless name *-Amen*

Please write at least three key things concerning your thoughts, resolutions, and corresponding actions to ensure clarity on suspicion and lack of trust.

Thoughts

1.____

2____

3____

Resolutions

1____

2.____

3____

Action to be taken

1____

2____

3____

10

SEX IN MARRIAGE

For many, marriage is a beautiful experience, and having a beautiful, blissful marriage is a decision. One of the things that makes marriage beautiful is that it provides the right and legitimate foundation for companionship. The husband and wife have each other and should enjoy and price being together highly. Sex is an integral part of marriage, and it is a vital part of the union. Sex is not only for pro-creation but also for companionship and pleasure. A marriage is consummated by sex between the husband and wife, and sex is both a spiritual and physical ritual; it is sacred, and it is a covenant between a man and woman who are married.

> **Sex is an integral part of marriage, and it is a vital part of the union. Sex is not only for pro-creation but also for companionship and pleasure.**
> **A marriage is consummated by sex between the husband and wife, and sex is both a spiritual and physical ritual; it is sacred, and it is a covenant between a man and woman who are married.**

However, it may interest you to know that even when you are not married, everyone you have sexual intercourse with you entered a covenant with, knowingly or unknowingly, and this is a blood covenant. Blood covenant is the highest form of a covenant you can have; it signifies the unification of life, which is spiritual. There is nothing like casual sex or fling; once is enough to cut the blood covenant.

Sex is for marriage, but marriage is not for sex. By implication, SEX IS ALSO A FORM OF MARRIAGE. All other activities are ceremonies, which are also important in making the union formal and open so that other intending suitors do not trespass.

The wedding ceremony is a very important aspect of marriage and should not be undermined by any means. If you go ahead and start living with someone without the marriage ceremony, you are deemed to be living with someone you are not married to. Even if you have a quiver full of children together, you are still not married, and your children will be deemed out of wedlock. You must do the right thing, and no single individual has an exclusive interpretation of right or wrong; that is why norms, values, beliefs, and culture guide society; these are acceptable guidelines by which the members of society live their daily lives openly and relatively privately. However, the Word of God is a trusted guide.

With the above, for clarity in this context, we will define marriage as the union between a man and a woman that has both legal and spiritual backing and is formally recognised by the public and those in close association with the couple. This union is furthermore consummated in privacy by the husband and wife through sexual activities.

With the above, for clarity in this context, we will define marriage as the union between a man and a woman that has both legal and spiritual backing and is formally recognised by the public and those in close association with the couple. This union is furthermore consummated in privacy by the husband and wife through sexual activities.

For the Christian, in marriage, the husband and the wife are obligated to make themselves available for each other's sexual needs (**1 Corinthians 7:1-5). K** is **JV.**

It is a fraudulent act to refuse your spouse sex for a prolonged period, even to engage in spiritual activities like fasting. The husband or wife must seek the consent of his or her spouse before proceeding on a prolonged period of praying and fasting
(1 Corinthians 7:5) KJV.

It must be underscored in clear terms that marriage and sex are God's idea, and God understands how powerful emotions can be; beyond recreation, it is perfectly normal for humans to be emotional and seek to fulfil their emotional needs, including sexual needs. However, these emotional needs that are erotic can only be fulfilled in a marriage relationship between a man and woman who are legitimately married.

What about those who are not married? They are to abstain from sex; any act of sex outside marriage is fornication or adultery. Sex is for marriage; it is expected that those who get married are two consenting adults; however, being adults and consenting does not give you a right to have sex even with another consenting adult; as long as you are not married, you are indulging in the act of fornication or adultery.

That is the truth of the matter based on the Bible. The Bible deals with other matters relating to sexual activity as it concerns same-sex relationships, homosexuality, sex with animals- bestiality, and several other details, including incest. This is not the focus of this book.

For the Christian, sex is an obligation akin to a debt owed to your spouse; this is as important as it can be. Sex is the one thing that you are not expected to get from anybody else on the earth but from each other as man and wife- referring to the generic Adam and Eve as representative of man and wife. It is neither for Adam and Steve nor Eve and Evelyn. In essence, this is to clarify that it is not for homosexuality nor Lesbianism and certainly not for the man or the woman with his or her best friend on four legs.

For the Christian, sex is an obligation akin to a debt owed to your spouse; this is as important as it can be. Sex is the one thing that you are not expected to get from anybody else on the earth but from each other as man and wife- referring to the generic Adam and Eve as representative of man and wife. It is neither for Adam and Steve nor Eve and Evelyn. In essence, this is to clarify that it is not for homosexuality nor Lesbianism and certainly not for the man or the woman with his or her best friend on four legs.

Holding this picture of sex as an obligation in mind, even when you are married to someone of a different faith (maybe you got married before becoming a Christian), the Christian husband or wife owes his wife or her husband an obligation to seek permission to abstain from sexual activities for a season to enable him or her engage in spiritual activities that may require abstinence.

So, a man or woman wants to give themselves to fasting for seven days; in my opinion, note, it's my opinion, as long as you break your fast each day in that seven days, you can have sex within the period of breaking your fast for that day. For example, you are fasting, and you break your fast by six pm daily; between six pm and twelve midnight that day, you can engage in sex if your spouse wants sex. Your fast begins after midnight for the next day.

This also concerns your convictions; as the Bible says, anything outside the faith is a sin. Seven days may be a long time for some spouses to abstain from sex, but it is fine to abstain from sex for the whole seven days straight if your spouse understands. I believe that will give you a sense of purity and sanctity for your spiritual exercise.

SEX AND PERSONAL HYGIENE

Sex is intimate, and our sexual organs are very private; until we grant our spouse access, it is entirely ours to keep and care for. Because of this, some people take it for granted and may not do what is necessary to ensure proper hygiene. No matter how you dress up and wear your perfume, you need to ensure that you keep the private parts of your body in good hygiene, whether you are single or married, even when you are celibate.

Your underwear is very important, and that goes for men and women. Cleaning and changing your bra, pants, sweatshirts, and boxers shorts is essential for your hygiene. The least is to have seven sets of Bras and eight pants; you will agree that this is quite modest. The men need a dozen since sometimes they cannot do their laundry as easily and frequently as the ladies. Some ladies pile up undies for several weeks before they wash them, and that is why I recommend a small number so you can wash them frequently and change them frequently, too. Make it a habit of washing your underwear when you bathe at night. I recommend hand washing for ladies' pants and bras so you can focus on sensitive areas. I also recommend changing them every six months, especially for your pants.

Storing undies, especially pants, for a long period before laundry can affect their wear and tear. It may make them prone to bacterial infection, especially where there may have been viginal discharge left on them.

I know many women may not be able to change their bras every six months, not because they can not afford it but because sometimes, even when they have a dozen new bras, there is always just this one or two sets that work better with our bodies and may sit well with nearly everything we wear. Sometimes, it's just the colour or the cut or design. (Some of us are guilty as charged)

Part of personal hygiene is to shave those private areas; if you are prone to having bumps, it is recommended to trim the pubic hair low rather than completely shaving the whole hair off. Shaving reduces the possibility of bacteria growing in that area since it is often covered and maybe a bit warmer than other exposed parts of the body. (a doctor told me this)

Shaving or trimming the pubic hair may also make the area a lot more convenient during intercourse, which may involve a lot of friction and skin-to-skin interactions. Sometimes, growing long pubic hair may lead to blisters and pain during intercourse.

Ladies, they are advised to keep the natural flora of the vagina, which is vital for the self-cleansing mechanism that works naturally inside. Inserting chemical cleansing agents and vaginal douche is not recommended as it may interact with good bacteria and make one prone to recurrent infection. Some people believe that eating certain kinds of food can affect the odour of the vagina (I recommend you do your research on this if you think the odour of your private part is unpleasant or offensive)

Another important area is cleansing after using the restroom; except for other reasons, it is not advisable to wash with water, where you cannot wipe dry with a towel. So, in the comfort of your home, where you have access to a proper towel, you can wash with water every time you use the restroom.

Still, wiping with a disposable towel or tissue is highly recommended when you are away from the convenience of using towels to wipe dry after washing with water. This is because if you do not wipe dry, washing will leave the area wet, and with no air going into the area, it will likely generate an unpleasant odour and create a convenient environment for bacteria to thrive.

During sex, it is important to use the right lubricants to moisten that area for better frequency during the exchange of thrusting and receiving. This may also enhance pleasure, increase satisfaction, and aid orgasm. The issue is, you cannot use just any lubricant as that may lead to infection and may even inhibit pregnancy in some cases (please do your research or speak with a specialist on what lubricants to use)

SEX AND INFECTION

Infection can be a fallout of poor personal hygiene; it may result from having a foreign body in your Vigina, especially family planning devices, and it may also be sexually transmitted. Whatever the cause of an infection, it is important to deal with your spouse with maturity when handling issues relating to infection in marriage. Trust is a key requirement for a happy marriage when dealing with your spouse. When you notice there may have been an infection after sexual intercourse with your spouse, the first thing you should do is discuss it and find a solution to it.

It is dangerous to assume or to conclude that the infection came because your spouse has been unfaithful. Do not cast away trust on assumptions; this is a sensitive subject and can break a good marriage, but this should not be the case when dealing with your spouse. Ladies are more prone to contracting infection because of their biological makeup. There are a lot of bacteria and fungal elements running around, and if one is not careful, one may judge the spouse who got an infection from the environment and spoil their marriage or sex life.

A lady can get an infection from just squatting over an office toilet facility for a pee in three minutes. That infection can be sexually transmitted to her spouse during intercourse. This does not mean her hygiene is compromised or she is unfaithful or wayward.

A Lady who has a family planning procedure that involves the insertion of a foreign object in her body is believed to be more susceptible to infection from the environment as the presence of the foreign body, such as coil, copper T and others, already caused a compromise in her system and may deplete her immune system. Bearing this in mind, if her husband has or is seeing someone else or had other sexual partners, she is more likely to get an infection than any of the parties involved because of the presence of the foreign body in the person. (a doctor explained this to me)

Childbirth and other hormonal changes in a woman's body can lead to changes that may deplete her immune system and make her prone to infection.

Often, in some parts of the world, many people do not do routine checks on their health, except if it is a mandatory exercise from their workplace, e.g. as a nurse or medical practitioner. As a result, an infection can stay very long in a person's body long enough to cause a compromise in their immune system and become chronic and resistant to regular treatments with antibiotics or antifungals. The person may be required to have a complete change in their diet and even lifestyle. This may be necessary for a recurrent yeast infection, requiring a change in diet, eating foods without yeast, and eating more vegetables that can boost the body's alkaline ratio and immunity. (please consult your doctor and do your research.

SEX AND PLEASURE

I believe God has designed the vagina for all the purposes it was created for; sex, pleasure, and procreation. When properly stimulated under the right circumstances, foreplay can go a long way to help stimulate the right hormones that will make the vagina favourable and conducive for receiving her partner. Just as nature programs it to dilate to the required centimetres when it's time to get a baby out, there is a natural program that prepares her to receive her partner if the right stimulus is applied.

We all have our love language, and for many ladies, foreplay starts long before the bedroom; it could be a kind word, a kind gesture, a word of encouragement, a text message, or even helping with the house chores. Understand yourselves and find your trigger button; it goes a long way to make sex a lot more pleasurable and satisfying.

Men also have turn-on and turn-off buttons. I know men are turned on by respect, good hygiene, good looks, and much more. Many are also turned off by disrespect, rudeness, and dirty ladies. All of this is within the context of marriage. (because I can feel the vibes of some ladies saying, why do they visit prostitutes and get infections if they care about hygiene and cleanliness?) That is another day's discussion. But I can tell you for free, for some men, all they want is a hole when they are in heat. That does not make it right; as a person, it is important to set healthy boundaries in every area of your life. Moderation and balance are the watchwords.

SEX AND ORGASM

Often, it is believed that most men get to orgasm during sex, while a lot of women are assumed never to get there. It is interesting to know that a handful of men care about taking their wives to paradise on every ride; while that is a good intention, it is often a function of one's disposition. Some women have cheated themselves into not enjoying sex and getting the pleasure that comes with it because of some myths, narratives, and stereotypes they've filled their minds with, most of which, even though not communicated verbatim, have been an integral part of the society they grew up in, from believing that sex is for procreation and not pleasure. Some others believe that if they respond in a way that shows they are enjoying sex, their spouse might become proud and weaponise sex.

Yet, some believe that they may be considered indecent and sexually corrupt if they engage their spouse in how to pleasure them.

On this matter of sex, you must understand that sex is God's idea, and God put all those organs in the right place for pleasure, companionship, and procreation.

Let me sound this here: there is no sex in heaven because we will not require our gender and physical bodies to do anything in heaven; our bodies are like the house given to us to enable us to function on this earth and in this life, so if you do not enjoy the act of sex in your marriage on this earth; you will never know what it feels like to get to paradise (orgasm) because it would not happen in heaven.

> Let me sound this here: there is no sex in heaven because we will not require our gender and physical bodies to do anything in heaven; our bodies are like the house given to us to enable us to function on this earth and in this life, so if you do not enjoy the act of sex in your marriage on this earth; you will never know what it feels like to get to paradise (orgasm) because it would not happen in heaven.

What even makes it paradise is the legality of the ritual. The only legitimate place to enjoy sex without a sense of guilt is in marriage, so enjoy it. Your libido may be at different points on the bar; I strongly advise that husband and wife discuss their sexual expectations; this should include pleasure points, treasure hunt, trigger buttons, and everything in between, including their sexual fantasies, and find a middle ground for your sex life and pleasure. Some of these fantasies may be extreme, but use God's word to find a balance and not blackmail or condemn yourselves. I mean, two things cannot happen to you at the same time; after a hard day's job, the quickest and most effective therapy to give you a good sleep is sex therapy; it is cheap, affordable, and accessible as long as your spouse is only a roll away. If you don't get it, please read it again.

You must be involved and engaged in sex with your spouse, spirit, soul, and body, and thank God every time you have to have this therapy; it is within the boundaries of your marriage. Come to think of it, how much time does it take to have good sex therapy? As long as it requires for those on the ride together to get to paradise, it could be short or long; the most important thing is that both of you are in sync and arrive at your destination safely.

If, for some reason, someone didn't get there on time, then it will be fair for their partner to assist that one to cum-to-paradise. Orgasm is therapeutic and works for your mind and your body.

There are potential health benefits of orgasm. During sexual intercourse with your spouse, when you achieve orgasm, the body releases the hormone called oxytocin; this hormone is believed to be beneficial in regulating anxiety, which is believed to help in reducing the risk of heart disease, reducing the risk of cancer, such as ovarian cancer and helps you get better sleep. During sexual intercourse and the husband achieves orgasm and ejaculation, it is believed also to reduce the risk of prostate cancer. (Obviously, those engaging in sexual intercourse as husband and wife must be in good health, strong enough to cover the mileage they choose without recourse to artificial stimulants.)

Please don't go and drink something that will keep you standing erect for hours; this thing has no end; if you don't hit the notes today, tomorrow is another day. On a more serious note, if you think you are not doing very well in that department as a man, it might surprise you to know that, for some ladies, sexual satisfaction is not all about penetrative sex but how you treat them even outside the other room, love, care, conversations, kindness, support, and foreplay when you eventually get to the other room 😉 (my phone brought out a wink emoji, this life is virtual)

Understand your love language and make the best of this mystery called sex.

Sex is good for your marriage and your body, except where there are underlying conditions that may require abstinence. It is strongly advised that married couples should engage in sexual intercourse on average three to four days a week; what is important in this is that they both engage their minds and bodies and are determined to have pleasure and satisfy each other when doing so. Remember, sex is for marriage, marriage is not for sex, and sex does not guarantee a good marriage, but the subject of sex can contribute to the breaking of a seemingly good marriage.

LIBIDO BAR

In Marriage, the husband and wife may not be at par on the libido bar. However, both of you need to be patient with each other and find a middle ground for your sexual needs.

In Marriage, the husband and wife may not be at par on the libido bar. However, both of you need to be patient with each other and find a middle ground for your sexual needs.

You can bring yourselves up to par in your sex life as a married couple. Another interesting postulation is that the female body is naturally structured to enable her to have pleasure and reach orgasm in many different ways, from her nipples and clitoris to her vagina; she can enjoy and should enjoy sex and orgasm if she puts her mind to it and engages her body in the act, of course, the help of her husband is required in this transaction.

Come to think of it, the mere thought of a woman's body can stimulate a man to the point of orgasm, and when he finally settles in to touch, caress, and work himself through the horizontal and vertical zones of her body, orgasm is almost always guaranteed. So, the woman that has that power and prowess will now not enjoy the ride? I think it's unfair; that is the reason every married woman must decide to enjoy, derive pleasure, and arrive at paradise during sexual intercourse with her husband. It starts with a decision first; everything else can be fixed.

DO NOT WEAPONIZE SEX

During sexual intercourse, we can be vulnerable with whom we engage in the act; it's so private and sacred that I cringe at the thought of anyone who is married relishing and engaging in this ritual with anyone else except their spouse. That is the lowest point you can go. In a sense, whoever you engage in sex with, you have trusted with your life; you have given power over your life.

Sex is spiritual, and even if you call someone your sex slave because you can overpower them physically, in the real sense of it, you are their captive spiritually.

If you do not find it appropriate to be naked in the presence of family and friends, why would you find it comfortable having flings or casual sex with people you do not want to be seen with in public? Such as a prostitute or pimp, a maid, or your house help, male or female? This sacred thing, called sex, can be a thing of joy and fulfilment in its right place- marriage and yet it can be someone's undoing when misplaced. It is legitimate in marriage with your spouse and shameful with anyone else.

Sex is too sacred, personal, and intimate to be seen as a fun activity or trivialised as a game. It is a weakness to try to use sex as a way to control, humiliate, or manoeuvre someone. It is a loud statement of one's moral bankruptcy, insecurity, sensual weakness, and internal system failure on a spiritual, mental, and physical scale.

A Christian who seeks to weaponise sex against their spouse has fallen from grace, lacks an understanding of what it means to be married, and does not understand the one flesh theory on which all other principles of marriage hinge. The lack of knowledge will bring about the forfeiture of many graces without a fight. Remember, the Bible says; one will chase a thousand and two ten thousand. There is no better place to put this to work than in marriage, based on the one flesh theory, knowing that the same power that joins you and Christ together joins you two as husband and wife. The Apostle Paul calls this a mystery and says: "… I speak concerning Christ and His church." The same principle holds: the husband is the head of his wife, as Christ is the head of the church. (Ephesians 5:31-32).

When you deny your spouse sex for any reason, note I used the word deny, which is different from abstain when you deny your spouse sex for reasons other than health concerns and for short periods to give yourself to spiritual exercise; you have weaponised sex and may be using it as a measure of control or punishment; this is not just bad or wrong, but it is summarised as a misdemeanour in your marriage, as the Bible describes the one who does that as a fraud. (1 Corinthians 7:5). You know that, by all standards, your spouse cannot and should not consider sex outside marriage, and then you weaponised sex to punish, manipulate and control the one you pledged and vow to love the rest of your life. It is so easy to think of this as a light matter, but it is not, and by doing so, you are dealing treacherously with your spouse, and God says, for dealing with your spouse treacherously, your prayers will not be answered.

Read Malachi 2:12-17 (for those who do not have access to a Bible, I have inserted five verses from the Amplified Classic Translation.

Malachi 2:12-17

The Lord will cast out of the tents of Jacob to the last man those who do this [evil thing], the Master and the servant [or the pupil] alike, even him who brings an offering to the Lord of hosts.

And this you do with double guilt; you cover the altar of the Lord with tears [shed by your unoffending wives, divorced by you that you might take heathen wives], and with [your own] weeping and crying out because the Lord does not regard your offering any more or accept it with favour at your hand.

Yet you ask, Why does He reject it? Because the Lord was witness [to the covenant made at your marriage] between you and the wife of your youth, against whom you have dealt treacherously and to whom you were faithless. Yet she is your companion and the wife of your covenant [made by your marriage vows].

And did not God make [you and your wife] one [flesh]? Did not One make you and preserve your spirit alive? And why [did God make you two] one? Because He sought a godly offspring [from your union]. Therefore, take heed to yourselves, and let no one deal treacherously and be faithless to the wife of his youth.

For the Lord, the God of Israel, says: I hate divorce and marital Separation and him who covers his garment [his wife] with violence. Therefore, keep a watch upon your spirit [that it may be controlled by My Spirit], that you deal not treacherously and faithlessly [with your marriage mate].

You have wearied the Lord with your words. Yet you say, In what way have we wearied Him? [You do it when by your actions] you say, Everyone who does evil is good in the sight of the Lord, and He delights in them. Or [by asking], Where is the God of justice?

The above summarises for all intent what you do against your wife or husband by extension, whether you divorce her or him or deny him or her their conjugal rights by refusing to have sex with your spouse, except on health grounds or may be grounds of adultery, not suspected adultery but adultery, and only if you think that divorce is the only option.

Note, if you deny your spouse sex intending to make them vulnerable to committing adultery, and they eventually commit adultery, you partake of their sins because you made yourself a stumbling block, causing someone to fall, even though your spouse will bear the consequences.

I deliberately chose the AMPC edition to cover all the extensions and objections anyone may raise. We must understand the implications of the ONE FLESH theory in marriage; anything that wrongfully separates the one flesh is equivalent to divorce. One of the definitions of divorce is to dissociate or separate something or someone from another, usually with an undesirable effect.

Sex is a binding force, a joining force, and a spiritual activity akin to a ritual that fuels the flames of love between the married couple and cements their vows.

Sex is a binding force, a joining force, and a spiritual activity akin to a ritual that fuels the flames of love between the married couple and cements their vows.

In marriage, once sex is removed from the equation, even though all other activities remain, the relationship can be compared to an ordinary one. Sex is an obligation and, by extension, a duty in marriage for the two that have become one flesh in that union, and you cannot divorce sex from marriage.

Whether you are seeing someone else is not the issue; you can be under the same roof and be technically divorced if sex is not in your marriage for a prolonged period, and by so doing, you are dealing treacherously with your spouse. If husband and wife live far apart by choice and can maintain their purity, it is excusable but not ideal.

So, husband or wife, leave your offering at the altar, wipe your tears, and go and reconcile with the spouse you married so that your prayers are no longer hindered. We Must give attention to the word of God in all honesty so we do not bring hardship to our lives with our own hands.

So, husband or wife, leave your offering at the altar, wipe your tears, and go and reconcile with the spouse you married so that your prayers are no longer hindered. We Must give attention to the word of God in all honesty so we do not bring hardship to our lives with our own hands.

You may have good reasons for taking a stand, such as denying your spouse sex; my question to you is, when did God's word become a question of reasoning? Often, God's word is the complete opposite of reason, and that is where the power is; when we obey God's word despite reasoning, we activate the power of God in our life and situation, and that can produce a ripple effect causing changes in many other areas of our life, including our health, finances and total well being; this too is a mystery, but I speak concerning God's word.

Malachi 2:16 refers to the wife as a garment; this has enormous spiritual implications (discussion for another day). The wife is a covering for her husband, and every time the husband deals treacherously with the wife, he exposes himself and becomes vulnerable to attacks of different sorts and sources. The Bible says you cover your garment with violence; let us not even start to discuss those wife-beaters here. Please deal generously and lovingly with the wife of your youth and practice your Christian faith in your marriage with the wife of your youth. There are many benefits to it.

MARRIAGE IS A MYSTERY, AND SEX VALIDATES IT

Marriage is still a mystery today; the synergy it creates can be far-reaching. Imagine, one will chase a thousand and two ten thousand; that is why multiple forces fight against marriages today. Imagine governments enacting laws to discourage young ladies from committing to marriage; they promise child support when you have a child outside wedlock. In most cases, the child does not take on the man's name, so a young lady has three children for three different men. What a world. The governments in different parts of the world are trying very hard to make light and trivialise the sanctity of marriage. They started several hundreds of years ago (read about Plato's proposition on children of the state)

Today, many forces come against marriages, even in subtle ways, such as grudges, bitterness, unforgiveness, and so many other issues that Christians should ordinarily not struggle with. Soon enough, they take it out on their spouse by denying them sex and then, thinking how they could have survived this long without it, they must be seeing someone, and they allow the devil to run a rampage in their marriage. By so doing, they are poisoning the minds of their children and those around them about marriage, leaving them thinking that marriage is not a thing of joy; it's such a destructive cycle. Whatever you do, please do not weaponise sex, and do not use your sexual powers or prowess to manipulate or punish your spouse; this, too, is a form of witchcraft.

If there are genuine concerns, instead of denying your spouse sex, please discuss them with your spouse and prayerfully resolve them. This, too, shall pass away.

ACTION NOTE/CHECKLIST

1. Be intentional about your sex life in marriage- plan for it and go for it.

2. Where there are disparities in libido ratio- discuss the frequency and meet yourselves halfway.

3. Therapists recommend that having sex an average of three or four times a week is a good activity for a healthy marriage.

4. Understand yourselves and help each other make the best of it and get satisfaction.

5. People generally have their love language, and love nodes talk about it and maximise it

6. Women generally may require foreplay to prepare them mentally- this may begin from way long before the bedroom.

7. Be content with your spouse and be flexible; you can help each other spice things up occasionally. Most of the missionaries have long gone.

8. If you are uncomfortable with anything, discuss it and find a solution to it; you are in this together

9. Sexual interest may diminish with age, activities, and responsibilities; find ways to fan the flames and keep the courtship high.

10. Be conscious of each other's health needs and make adjustments where necessary. Every battle can be won by a united force with God's help.

PRAYER

Dear heavenly Father, thank you for giving me a spouse who is yielded to your word; together, we will keep the bond of fellowship in marriage by following your word.

In the Matchless name of Jesus – *Amen.*

Please write at least three key things that concern your thoughts, resolutions, and corresponding actions to bring your sex life up to par with one another.

Thoughts

1._______________________________

2_______________________________

3_______________________________

Resolutions

1_______________________________

2._______________________________

3_______________________________

Action to be taken

1_______________________________

2_______________________________

3_______________________________

11

DEALING WITH INFIDELITY IN MARRIAGE

Marriage is a beautiful experience for many people; many go into marriage with expectations. Except in rare cases, I am not sure if anyone goes into marriage intending to commit adultery. Many people go into marriage with a mindset to settle down, which may refer to settling down with one person as a life partner and a sexual partner. Unfortunately, statistics from the Institute for Family Studies in a study carried out in 2010 and 2016 showed that men are more likely to cheat than women, with twenty per cent of men and thirteen per cent of women reporting having sex with someone other than their partner while still married.

Love is a decision, and infidelity is a decision; we all choose how we live our lives; by choosing not to be faithful and committing infidelity, we have decided to go against God's word.

These statistics are not biblical, nor does the Bible recommend them, and should not be used as excuses for defiling your marriage bed.

Love is a decision, and infidelity is a decision; we all choose how we live our lives; by choosing not to be faithful and committing infidelity, we have decided to go against God's word.

Infidelity is defined as a violation of a couple's emotional and or/sexual exclusivity that commonly results in feelings of anger, sexual jealousy, and rivalry. (Wikipedia) . Wikipedia also says infidelity is synonymous with cheating, straying, adultery, unfaithfulness, two-timing, or having an affair.

ADULTERY IN MARRIAGE

For clarity, we will focus on Adultery in Marriage as the extreme of infidelity. There is no doubt that upon getting married, it is an expectation for both parties to understand that in marital relationships, exclusivity is commonly assumed as a boundary for a sexual relationship. In light of the above, it is within the limits of our Christianity and values to know that adultery is a sin against God, the body of Christ, your spouse, the Holy Spirit who dwells in you, and your spirit. It is a spiritual sin well addressed in the Bible; you sin against your body. We will, however, explore some of the circumstances and situations that may lead to Adultery in marriage.

As couples grow older, sometimes their sexual needs diminish, and being burdened with additional responsibilities can also affect the husband and wife differently. For example, sometimes, the lack of pregnancy early enough can make the woman more demanding of sex, especially during her ovulation periods, while this may be a turn-off for some men who may be feeling controlled and manipulated. Understanding your spouse's desperation for a child is essential, especially when she feels her biological clock is ticking.

And then a baby comes, bringing with it joys and challenges. The presence of a newborn or young child can deplete a woman's libido drastically, primarily because of the stress and sometimes post-partum depression; the changes in her body physically and internally can be traumatic for her. This leads to a sharp decline from the once sexually active woman to one who now gets easily irritated even by her husband's touch.

These and many more are a handful of challenges that can affect a woman's sexuality.

On the other hand, the increase in financial responsibilities as the family grows can also be a concern for the husband, which may affect his sexual drive/desires negatively. Many may also be going through a mid-life crisis and specific challenges in life. Mid-life crisis happens to both men and women. Still, it is more apparent in men, especially in a male-dominated society like most of Africa, where the success of the man in the area of finances and status is a validation for him as a man.

The expectations of success and the parameters by which success is measured are also a source of concern. For example, a man should have built his own house at a certain age, ensured his children were catered to, and attended certain schools that defined the social status of men of his calibre. Sometimes, incidents may drastically affect a man's career progression, and if he had not put measures in place, he might not have been able to get back on his feet and pursue his dreams. These issues are often not addressed, but we must have these conversations and find a way to support each other.

All these and more may lead to dissatisfaction and culminate in unfulfillment in marriage, which may flow into other areas of the relationship if not dealt with firmly and urgently. The biggest challenge is the disappointment that comes with these changes, where one party feels more on the receiving end and may not have been prepared to support their partner. The natural response is fight or flight as an escape route, leading to further disconnection.

Married people should be open to conversations, discuss their challenges, and find ways to support themselves through challenging times. We must find our security in God and respect each other in times when we are vulnerable. There is too much secrecy between couples today, and it is because of insecurity.

Sometimes, a woman only discovers the man has challenges at work or with his business when it is too late; sometimes, it is from a third party; this is unacceptable. Being vulnerable in a union bound by love and vows is okay; we must learn to trust our spouse and support each other so our spouse can avoid running into the wrong hands for respite and support.

Everyone needs a support system, even more importantly in times of vulnerability. If you do not resolve to be each other's go-to person as a couple, you both risk falling into a triangular relationship. Where there is a third party holding your best secrets and nursing your inner pains, this third party could be a friend, sibling, uncle, mother or father, and that doesn't make it right. One day, they could use your best-kept secret against you.

Sometimes, the other party runs to the wrong person, predominantly because of insecurity and dissatisfaction. Such dissatisfaction can breed unhealthy relationships outside the home for the dis-satisfied partner, who may seek emotional respite in the wrong places; this, in turn, may give way to adultery, which is not only a sin against your spouse but against your body and God. The Christian man or woman should not entertain any thought of adultery and fornication. It is a sin and an evil act (1 Corinthians 6:18-20). The Message translation puts it this way.

> *"There's more to sex than mere skin on skin. Sex is as much a spiritual mystery as a physical fact. As written in Scripture, "The two become one." Since we want to become spiritually one with the Master, we must not pursue the kind of sex that avoids commitment and intimacy, leaving us more lonely than ever—the kind of sex that can never "become one." There is a sense in which sexual sins*

are different from all others. In sexual sin we violate the sacredness of our bodies, these bodies that were made for God-given and God-modeled love, for "becoming one" with another. Or didn't you realise that your body is a sacred place, the place of the Holy Spirit? Don't you see that you can't live however you please, squandering what God paid such a high price for? The physical part of you is not some piece of property belonging to the spiritual part of you. God owns the whole works. So let people see God in and through your body."
1 Corinthians 6:14-20. Message Translation

The word adultery appears about forty times in the Bible and is well-addressed as a sin. No faithful Christian will seek justification for committing adultery. Adultery and fornication refer to sexual sin and can be used interchangeably. Adultery is often used when one or both parties involved in sexual sin are married; fornication, on the other hand, may be used when one or both parties involved in sexual sin are singles.

"but who so commits adultery with a woman lacks understanding: he that does it destroys his own soul"
(proverbs 6:32-35)

Verse thirty-three says

"A wound and dishonour shall he get; and his reproach shall not be wiped away."

There are spiritual implications for adultery. A man who commits adultery makes himself vulnerable to spiritual attacks, which may manifest in different areas of his life, including poverty, sickness, bitterness of mind and soul, and hardship. Do not forget the health implications; he is more exposed to contracting sexually transmitted diseases and, worse still, passing it on to your spouse; such activities are a wicked act; many have been carried away captives and have opened themselves to demonic attacks through sexual sins. Remember, sex is both a spiritual and physical act; in fact, it is a ritual of some sort.

That means sexual intercourse is one of the quickest and surest ways to a person's spirit. If done outside the boundaries of marriage, it can expose someone to demonic influence and oppression, just like anger, bitterness, unforgiveness, and seeking vengeance or being vindictive can also expose someone to demonic influence. Adultery is bondage for the one who practices it; for whatever reasons one indulges in the act, it is bondage for those who indulge in the act because they have the means, especially the men who patronise prostitutes or other ladies. After all, they have money; it is still a bondage, to the extent that no matter how much money they have, they will never be satisfied and will keep seeking joy and happiness that may elude them for life. Sex is not a game or sport you engage in with different people. Be content with your spouse, and be loyal and committed to your spouse in marriage. Committing adultery is giving your strength to strangers and scattering your seeds as a man.

The Bible describes a woman who commits adultery as a wicked woman who lies in wait to capture her prey. You will never be better or blessed for it. You submit yourself to rape when you commit adultery or fornication as a woman. A married woman involved in adultery and fornication can cut short her life and the life of her husband and children. Please do not have anything to do with adultery and fornication nor have pleasure in them that do so.

The Bible describes a woman who commits adultery as a wicked woman who lies in wait to capture her prey. You will never be better or blessed for it. You submit yourself to rape when you commit adultery or fornication as a woman. A married woman involved in adultery and fornication can cut short her life and the life of her husband and children. Please do not have anything to do with adultery and fornication nor have pleasure in them that do so.

The mystery is that, often, those who do it, even though they know it is wrong, do not drink the cup once but continue in it until their conscience dies; that is the real bondage: no remorse, no

The implications of sexual sins transcend marriage, gender, and race; many people, especially ladies, are unable to keep a home in marriage because of the sexual sins they committed even as single ladies. The consequences far outweigh the transient pleasures of a night full of rumbles if you can go all the nine yards.

repentance; instead, they seek justification. Adultery is not a means to an end or an end in itself.

The implications of sexual sins transcend marriage, gender, and race; many people, especially ladies, are unable to keep a home in marriage because of the sexual sins they committed even as single ladies. The consequences far outweigh the transient pleasures of a night full of rumbles if you can go all the nine yards.

ADULTERY CAN BE FORGIVEN

If you have found yourself in this situation or you know someone who has, please let them know that adultery should not be the end of their marriage. It may interest you to know that Jesus addressed the issue of adultery. As we read in Mark, chapter ten from verse eleven

"Whosoever shall put away their spouse to marry another commits adultery" (Mark 10:11-12). Let us read it in the amplified classic translation.

Mark 10:2-12 AMPC

"And some Pharisees came up, and, to test Him and try to find a weakness in Him, asked, Is it lawful for a man to dismiss and repudiate and divorce his wife?

He answered them, What did Moses command you?

They replied Moses allowed a man to write a bill of divorce and to put her away.

But Jesus said to them, Because of your hardness of heart [your condition of insensibility to the call of God], he wrote you this precept in your Law.

But from the beginning of creation, God made them male and female.

*For this reason, a man shall leave [behind] his father and
his mother and be joined to his wife and cleave closely to her
permanently,*

*And the two shall become one flesh, so they are no longer two, but
one flesh.*

*What, therefore, God has united (joined together), let not man
separate or divide.*

And indoors, the disciples questioned Him again about this subject.

*And He said to them, Whoever dismisses (repudiates and divorces)
his wife and marries another commits adultery against her;*

*And if a woman dismisses (repudiates and divorces) her husband
and marries another, she commits adultery."*

Let us read the above verse in context; in verse two, the Pharisees came
to Jesus and asked him, is it lawful for a man to put away his wife?
Addressing the matter from the known to the unknown, he asked them
what the Law of Moses commanded. To which they answered that Moses
permitted them to serve the spouse a bill of divorce and put the person
away or leave (it is implied both ways)

Verse five says: "And Jesus answered and said unto them, For the hardness
of your heart he wrote you this precept." Verse six says, "But from the
beginning of the creation, God made them male and female." Verse seven,
"For this cause shall a man leave his father and mother, and cleave to his
wife" Verse eight," And they Twain shall be one flesh: so then they are
no more Twain, but one flesh" Verse nine "what therefore God has joined
together, let not man put asunder"

So, we see another light on the issue of adultery; the matter was so
disturbing to the disciples then, as it is to some people today, that when
they got home, his disciples brought up the topic again. Jesus clarifies
what he meant by the above explanation without mincing words.

Verse ten to twelve, "And in the house, his disciples asked him again. And he said unto them, whosoever shall put away his wife, and marry another, commits adultery against her. And if a woman shall put away her husband and be married to another, she commits adultery.

Now, I am aware that there are other cases in the Bible where Jesus has been quoted to say for the sake of fornication. But in this case, I want to believe that Jesus did not forget that one party could have been guilty of committing fornication against their spouse; that is why he puts the clause; Moses gave you the precept because of the hardness of your heart.

> If your heart is soft enough to forgive, and indeed it can be, you do not need to end your marriage on the grounds of fornication or adultery because even that is an act of adultery, and the Bible says God hates divorce.

If your heart is soft enough to forgive, and indeed it can be, you do not need to end your marriage on the grounds of fornication or adultery because even that is an act of adultery, and the Bible says God hates divorce.

With this in the background, let us look at how to manage adultery.

HOW TO MANAGE ADULTERY

Where a spouse has committed fornication or adultery, that person should own up to their mistakes, regardless of whatever excuse or reason they went into it. Come out, repent, and ask God for forgiveness. If your spouse is aware, apologise and ask for forgiveness, and God will give you the power to overcome it and live a life of purity in your marriage.

I have often said a Christian who commits adultery lacks an understanding of God's place in their life and does not hold God's word in high esteem. The Psalmist said, your word have I hid in my heart that I may not sin against you. They do not love and genuinely fear God. Adultery/fornication for the Christian is sacrilege. Your body is the temple of God, and the Holy Spirit lives in you; adultery/fornication is first a sin against God and then a sin against God's temple- where the Holy Spirit lives and a sin against your marriage and the one to whom you are married.

Understanding that your body is the temple of the Holy Spirit that dwells in you is the real deal, and that will keep you out of trouble; adultery and fornication is trouble, yes! There can be trouble in paradise.

> **The real reason for not committing adultery or fornication is because you have been bought with a price, not with corruptible elements like silver and gold, but with the precious blood of the Lord Jesus Christ, to whom you have now been joined as one spirit.**

The real reason for not committing adultery or fornication is because you have been bought with a price, not with corruptible elements like silver and gold, but with the precious blood of the Lord Jesus Christ, to whom you have now been joined as one spirit.

YOU DO NOT OWN YOUR BODY; IT BELONGS TO GOD, AND ONLY GOD AND THE ONE YOU ARE MARRIED TO CAN HAVE ACCESS TO YOUR BODY BECAUSE YOU ARE NOW ONE FLESH WITH THAT PERSON AND ONE SPIRIT WITH GOD.
(1 Corinthians 6:17)

So why forgive adultery?

As Christians, you do not deal with your spouse from a standing of what they did to you- instead, you align with God's word to deal with every situation in your life, including your marriage and your spouse. Whatever your spouse may have done does not require you to take action against them to the point of going against God's word and God's will for your life. When dealing with your spouse, I implore you to act in covenant kindness towards them. Your spouse has become one with you, one flesh, the same power that joins you to the Lord Jesus Christ joins you both together as husband and wife.

Do not allow the mistakes of others to lead you into trouble with God and cause a shipwreck in your faith and, eventually, your life. There may be many other reasons a couple or one person in the marriage may seek divorce.

I pray that you do not get to that point, but if it is for the issue of fornication or adultery, I hope you find a place in your heart to forgive, whether forgiveness is sought or not. Let me emphasise here that forgiveness is a choice you make regardless of the standing of the other party because forgiveness is your right to peace and happiness; you cannot move on and truly find peace until you forgive, so why do you want to remain imprisoned and bound when the key to your happiness is in your hand? That key is called **FORGIVENESS**.

I pray that you do not get to that point, but if it is for the issue of fornication or adultery, I hope you find a place in your heart to forgive, whether forgiveness is sought or not. Let me emphasise here that forgiveness is a choice you make regardless of the standing of the other party because forgiveness is your right to peace and happiness; you cannot move on and truly find peace until you forgive, so why do you want to remain imprisoned and bound when the key to your happiness is in your hand? That key is called FORGIVENESS.

In my opinion, one of the biggest crises in marriage is infirmity or sickness and protracted ailment, leading to one party becoming invalid. It's a complex situation to be in. It just slowly takes the life out of the relationship. Pray against sickness and ill health as much as you pray against fornication, adultery, death, and other evils. A lot of marriages go through trying times. If we are determined to make it work, we can. Unite as a team with God against the onslaught of Satan against your marriage.

DEALING WITH RECURRENT CASES OF ADULTERY

And where a spouse repeatedly commits adultery and refuses to yield to God's word. If you feel under threat of disease and infection and emotionally bullied by the act that you cannot continue, at this point, we can call to action the recommendations of the Lord Jesus Christ as recorded in the book of Matthew, chapter eighteen from verse fifteen.

> *"If your brother or sister sins, point out their fault, just between the two of you. If they listen to you, you have won them over. But if they will not listen, take one or two others along so that every matter may be established by the testimony of two or three witnesses.' If they still refuse to listen, tell it to the church, and if they refuse to listen even to the church, treat them as you would a pagan or a tax collector."*
> **Matthew 18:15-17 (New International Version)**

The above is very simple: how would you treat a pagan? A pagan is not just an unbeliever but someone holding other religious beliefs. It is a serious place to be. So you must keep praying for that person even though you may distance yourself from the person; in your spouse's case, you may choose separation as a measure of tough love. I want to believe that if your spouse truly loves and respects you, they will repent and reach out for reconciliation, but if they do not. The hard truth is that you should be prepared for the worst. Your total well-being is important.

Interestingly, the message translation puts it differently and follows the above-mentioned school of thought. Let us look at it.

> *"If a fellow believer hurts you, go and tell him—work it out between the two of you. If he listens, you've made a friend. If he doesn't listen, then take one or two others along so that the presence of witnesses will keep things honest and try again. If he still doesn't listen, tell the church. If he doesn't listen to the church, you'll have to start over from scratch, confront him with the need for repentance, and offer God's forgiving love again.*
> ***Mathew 18:15-17 (Message Translation)***

Forgiveness is a profound subject in the Bible; we are all standing because of forgiveness. What a privilege to offer that same forgiveness to those we may find undeserving of it. It may be painful but fulfilling; herein is God's love made perfect.

If you choose to stay or leave, do not take any extra weight with you; leave them all behind. Truly forgive even if you never forget. Some lessons are not to be overlooked, but remembering them should not sting us like a knife if we have truly forgiven.

We are not to relate with those who may have hurt us like a contagious disease when we see them. But we reserve the right to admit or not admit them into our lives or space.

> **If you choose to stay or leave, do not take any extra weight with you; leave them all behind. Truly forgive even if you never forget. Some lessons are not to be overlooked, but remembering them should not sting us like a knife if we have truly forgiven.**

ACTION NOTE/CHECKLIST

1. Be guided by God's word, not your feelings or findings. It may be difficult, but not impossible.

2. Forgive and move on with your marriage where there is true repentance. This is important to ensure there is no repeat.

3. Do not pack up a good marriage because of fornication/adultery. The offender will bear the consequences with God; just stay out of God's way and in God's will.

4. Assess the situation in isolation and deal with the issue in its appropriate circumstance.

5. In the case of repeated issues of adultery, find the common denominator if possible and seek help in God's word and also see a family therapist.

6. Don't forget to show love to the offender who genuinely repents and never remind them about the situation.

7. Trust may have been broken, but you need a lot of trust to move forward, so trust again just because you can.

8. When you choose to stay, and it continues, it may help to use protection while you're working on it, but if you find it hurtful and affecting your spiritual, mental, or physical health, it may be helpful to seek separation.

PRAYER

Dear Heavenly Father, as it is written- your word have I hid in my heart that I may not sin against you. I've yielded to your word now and always. Help us, Lord, even as we go through this difficult time.

In Jesus' matchless name-*Amen.*

Please write at least three key things as they concern your thoughts, resolutions, and corresponding actions to ensure you manage the issues of adultery and fornication if they ever occur.

Thoughts

1.____

2____

3____

Resolutions

1____

2.____

3____

Action to be taken

1____

2____

3____

12

MENTAL HEALTH AND LOVE

Marriage can be very beautiful and yet challenging for different people. One thing is important in life and required in managing the challenges that life throws at us, whether in marriage, career or health. Being mentally stable is a basic requirement in facing and overcoming challenges. As I reminisce on the journey of over twenty-plus years I have been in a marriage, there have been hiccups on the way, and I have mixed feelings as I mirror some of my challenges against the challenges of some of my clients and close friends.

Amidst the tears, joys, and hopes, I am grateful to God. I remember speaking with a close friend who had been diagnosed with a deadly disease but was strong in the face of the monster of an illness and had a strong support system, especially in her spouse, who was willing to give all he had for her health.

She was so inspiring and encouraging all through her journey through managing that terminal disease. One day, as we spoke, I broke down crying as I told her how much I admired her strength, that facing a potential death sentence with that disease, she was so cheerful and undaunted.

Indeed, God will not allow what we cannot bear to come to us. If many of us could choose our battles and challenges, I'm almost sure no one would desire a deadly, ravaging disease to fight, no matter how much our faith may have grown.

Yesterday was the service of song for my good friend, who is almost ten years younger than I am, yes! She passed on to Glory. Today is my wedding anniversary, a remarkable milestone, but with no celebration. I wish my friend were still alive today, but I wondered how many words of encouragement I could have given her to help her fight her battle.

I said this to let you know that maybe where you are at in your marriage is not as fatal; it may not be terminal; find the courage to hope and look forward to a better tomorrow, for it is only those who are alive that can have hope and believe for a better tomorrow.

Yet I must warn you that you keep a tab on your mental health; only you know exactly where you are in your relationship and mental health journey. While we must encourage you for the best, please walk the path that keeps you stable.

Spiritually

Mentally

Physically

You must be categorically well in these three faculties to judge rightly, strategise, and work things out.

Often, I have suggested a separation first to analyse things and give your brain and heart some time to breathe and assess the scenarios and situation so you can make the proper judgment and choose your battles and instruments of combat.

Assess if you can win the war without inflicting wounds on your mind, soul, and body. Choose life and well-being rather than imaginary trophies and bloodshed. There is no point in proving by staying in an abusive and mentally destructive marriage if you eventually lose your mind, your sanity, and even your life.

Indeed, many have lost their lives while they're still breathing; when one gets to a point where they can no longer use their minds to make the right decisions for themselves and those who depend on them (like their children), then the battle has been lost.

Never catch yourself in that state, no, not ever; always weigh your actions and the actions of others; how do they affect you? What choices are you going to make moving forward? What lessons have you learned to help you take better actions and reactions? Who are the stakeholders? What is at stake here? What strategies can you apply immediately? How quickly can the strategies begin to yield dividends?

There are many questions to ask and answer, but be objective and confident to reason these things out. It's okay as humans to be afraid, but it is death to stop thinking and to hold on to a dead branch for support. Life happens, and we must take the reins and ride the storm to shore if the boat is sinking.

> **Indeed, many have lost their lives while they're still breathing; when one gets to a point where they can no longer use their minds to make the right decisions for themselves and those who depend on them (like their children), then the battle has been lost.**

AVOID NARCISSISTIC PEOPLE

As much as you can, avoid narcissistic people. A lot of people do not have self-awareness and empathy, and that is the first deficiency of a narcissist; some of them suffer from Narcissist Personality Disorder. A once-loving spouse can transition into a narcissist, so avoid being the victim of love that turns sour, especially when they start gaslighting you. It's my personal opinion; I think Narcissism is the height of being self-centred and a high-power sort of witchcraft, as the case may be.

Emotional bullying can be as bad as physical bullying, if not worse, because, with physical bullying and abuse, there may be physical scars to show and treat. The person may likely reach out to the victim emotionally. Still, with emotional abuse, there may be no words or physical scars, but injuries are inflicted on your heart and mind, which can lead to physical and mental ailments.

Avoid it at all costs, know your threshold and be mindful, be empathetic with yourself, be self-aware, and don't let anyone gaslight you to the point of brokenness and worthlessness. Be Relationship Intelligent.

One thing I have noticed is that when you are dealing with a Narcissist, your insecurity is their security, so they always work to keep you subject to them and under at all times. It's a difficult place to be. Another significant trait of a narcissist is they are never genuinely interested in any form of reconciliation or conflict resolution that will validate your relationship and lead you to a place of joy and bliss.

Narcissists would use mixed messages to control you; they are nasty, cold, insensitive, and manipulative. They gaslight you intensely, and once you begin to build your firewalls and find your coping mechanisms to manage their treatment, they drop a softball, suddenly become warm, or do something that will make you feel like things are turning alright again. They can tell when your hopes rise and become the same sinister person.

Many times, narcissists do not start as narcissists; they love-bomb you at the beginning and validate you; some may buy you a lot of gifts, openly express their love and admiration for you, and speak proudly of you as a spouse. But the moment their expectations are not met, like a switch, they turn off and become your biggest nightmare. Some of their common weaponry includes silent treatment, ghosting, denying you emotional supply like intimacy, shutting down the communication lines or using mono-syllables like 'yes', 'no', 'okay', 'I can hear you', etc.

There are different degrees to which the Narcissistic trait may be revealed in a person; often, it is a function of their social and financial standing at any point in their life. They want to be idolised once they are in a place of power and influence and are narcissistic and selfish.

They can go to any length to demean you and put you down, even in the presence of your children and close associates. Note this very important trait about narcissist: they thrive in mentally derailing you and making you feel like you are worthless, unintelligent and non-coherent, and this they do by making sure that all their communications to you are void of clarity.

Let us focus on dealing with a Narcissist for a moment. The moment you continue to show how insecure you are before them and how much you need them, they become emboldened to hurt you more. So, be confident, self-reliant, secure, look your best, put up a good front, and be responsible.

> **They can go to any length to demean you and put you down, even in the presence of your children and close associates. Note this very important trait about narcissist: they thrive in mentally derailing you and making you feel like you are worthless, unintelligent and non-coherent, and this they do by making sure that all their communications to you are void of clarity.**

One of the important steps to take is to cut off the supply from them. Take charge of your life, and become intentional and productive. Ignore their distractions and stop giving them any form of validation, e.g. words of affirmation. Do not patronise them, and do not accept their soft balls. Match their energy when it comes to making you feel irrelevant. Without saying a word to them, become your best at what you do and become the best version of yourself. Success is the sweetest revenge when dealing with a narcissist.

If you feel threatened, seek help.

KNOW WHEN TO SEEK HELP

We all need a support system; never burn your bridges if you can. In this journey called marriage, many people go in with hopes and high expectations, which is good, but never forget, human beings are very temperamental and may be swayed by many things. You must make excuses for people, especially your loved ones.

Whatever you do, know your threshold and seek help when you cannot carry on alone but seek help in the right places. When seeking help, you must have good intentions and ensure you do not demonise your spouse. Seek help from those you know are genuinely interested in your well-being and will not add any more trouble.

But I can tell you for free, if you are dealing with a Narcissistic person who is vindictive and proud, they like control, you may be on a long journey trying to resolve all your issues because the Narcissistic person does not genuinely seek resolution they thrive in chaos, they get their fulfilment from making sure their partner turned victim is not fulfilled, that is what qualifies them to be Narcissists. That is why it is a personality disorder.

Be brave and decisive on how far you want to go. Many people do not understand what they may be dealing with from the onset because they may be naïve and trusting to a fault. We all need to have Relationship Intelligence.

> **But I can tell you for free, if you are dealing with a Narcissistic person who is vindictive and proud, they like control, you may be on a long journey trying to resolve all your issues because the Narcissistic person does not genuinely seek resolution they thrive in chaos, they get their fulfilment from making sure their partner turned victim is not fulfilled, that is what qualifies them to be Narcissists. That is why it is a personality disorder.**

It would be best if you were very firm with what you wanted and actively participated in how things played out for you in your marriage from the beginning. The red flags are usually there, but often, people don't know how to interpret them. The only change acceptable to the Narcissist is compliance; you must carry out their bidding but not their changing. There's always a consequence for not doing their bidding, and they will push their narrative until everyone agrees with them. They believe those who do not agree with them do not understand them, and those who agree with them genuinely love them.

PHYSICAL AND MENTAL ABUSE

When there is physical abuse, please seek safety. One thing I have come to realise is that silence empowers the offender. Be mindful of your physical health, too. It is the person that is alive that can talk about marriage. It is not a do-or-die affair; be careful how you respond to your spouse and be mindful of how their reactions affect you.

Any action or inaction taken or not taken to inflict pain and injury on you mentally, physically, or emotionally is abuse.

Blaming your spouse is abuse, the silent treatment is abuse, and hitting you and doing nothing deliberately to gaslight you is abuse. Manipulating you verbally or non-verbally to the point of accepting responsibility for how they treat you is abuse. Consistently ignoring your calls and messages over a prolonged period is abuse. Not acknowledging your presence is abuse; ghosting is abuse.

Sometimes, physical and spiritual signs indicate that you must take a break from your marriage. Please do not ignore those signs; so many people who died in abusive marriages may have ignored those signs.

NOTE THESE SIGNS

Take note: when you are constantly in a state of fear and panic, you have the feeling of being unsafe with the person around you, and you feel a threat to your life, it may be a sign that you need to take a break and seek help.

Where the person has repeatedly told you that if one of you does not leave or die, there will be no peace nor a way forward, it may be a sign.

You may need a break when you constantly feel sick like the spirit of infirmity has taken over you just from the thought of the person being close by or hearing the person's voice.

Sometimes, these compelling feelings result from the accumulation of destructive energy from the constant troubles in your marriage. As a direct consequence, some negative forces have dominated that environment, which may lead to something fatal, including death, if not given attention.

Sometimes, these compelling feelings result from the accumulation of destructive energy from the constant troubles in your marriage. As a direct consequence, some negative forces have dominated that environment, which may lead to something fatal, including death, if not given attention.

It is better and safer to leave that environment for a while even if things can be worked out eventually, and this may take months and sometimes years, but there can still be a change with the intervention of God through prayers.

Many people continue to stay in an abusive marriage because of insecurity; some of them are insecure about their future, what people will say, where the next meal will come from, how many years they have invested in the marriage, and what will happen to the children—so many questions.

My advice is that you should start by identifying a place to go to and stay while you are hoping and trying to work things out, even if it is just for you to catch your breath and figure out if you can work things out and if eventually, things do not work out as you hoped for, also explore your exit plan as a second option.

SEEK HELP IN THE RIGHT PLACES

When seeking help, do not run to your close friends who may not be able to help you; you shouldn't be seen in questionable places.

Do not confide in people you can be vulnerable with, like an ex-lover or someone who has been crushing on you or whom you may have had a crush on. You will be setting yourself up for trouble, which is not a healthy choice.

Take some time to pray. Often, praying may be the most challenging thing to do in times of pain and uncertainty, yet it is not always in the length of the prayer or the multiplicity of words but in the depth and total trust in God. Cast all your cares on Him because He cares for you. You need love and care the most at this point, and knowing that God cares, truly and lovingly, can be very comforting and uplifting.

Even if you brought this upon yourself, He is God; He will never judge you and always love and care for you. Understand it; it is called covenant kindness. God is bound by His word to care for you, and He does care for you.

The Bible says that God will deliver the lawful captive. Isaiah 49:24-25

"Shall the prey be taken from the mighty, or the lawful captive delivered? But thus saith the LORD, Even the captives of the mighty shall be taken away, and the prey of the terrible shall be delivered: for I will contend with him that contendeth with thee, and I will save thy children."
Isaiah 49:24-25

Nobody has the right to violate another person because they are married.

Marriage is meant to be a place of security and a haven from the cynical world; marriage should provide a home, hope and shelter for you when you are weary, vulnerable and need time to reload. Marriage is not a death sentence.

> **Marriage is meant to be a place of security and a haven from the cynical world; marriage should provide a home, hope and shelter for you when you are weary, vulnerable and need time to reload. Marriage is not a death sentence.**

Remember, the Bible say, "For this course *(of oneness, not only of body but of spirit and soul)* shall a man leave his father and his mother and cleave to his wife.."

"what therefore God has joined together, let no man put asunder (not even those who are married to themselves)."

ACTION NOTE

a. Please, if you need to leave to be alive, by all means, leave your marriage.

b. Remember, your children would rather have you alive and well than know their father or mother killed you.

c. All your insecurity can only be dealt with when you face them.

d. You may never know the number of angels God has in place to help you until you reach out in faith.

e. Everything you need to succeed and blossom is inside you; it has been locked in by intimidation and fear, so walk out and sower.

f. While separated, if your partner extends an olive branch, be sure there is no risk of relapse before you return, so your last state is not worse than the earlier state.

g. Separation or divorce is not a sentence to hellfire. Though God hates Divorce, God has a calling on your life, and it is not God's perfect will for anyone to be killed by violence or pain in marriage to make heaven. Sometimes, some marriages are like hellfire already; walk out of such.

Yet God can fix any problem if the parties involved are willing and obedient. Two can only walk together when they are in agreement.

PRAYER

Dear Lord, you know how much I love you and want your perfect will for my life. Please help me know and do your perfect will, even as it concerns my predicament in marriage.

In Jesus' matchless name-Amen

Please write at least three key things as they concern your thoughts, resolutions, and corresponding actions to ensure you manage the issues of your mental health in Marriage.

Thoughts

1.______________________________________

2______________________________________

3______________________________________

Resolutions

1______________________________________

2.______________________________________

3______________________________________

Action to be taken

1______________________________________

2______________________________________

3______________________________________

FINAL WORDS

I have put my heart into writing this book; I hope you find some help as you work out your marriage, hoping to make it an example of a Christian marriage. Where God's word stands in every situation and circumstance. I pray earnestly that as we have expectations, and though there may be pitfalls in our journey in marriage, we may yet find the strength to keep loving our spouse in times when love may not have failed but may seem not to be enough, yet to love we must, because after all is said and done, love will see us through as God is love, and loving is living.

There is no end to knowledge, and if you find better ways to navigate the trials and storms in your marriage, please share with those around you and reach out to us.

There are genuine challenges in marriage, and the more we can reach out to those around us to offer comfort through good counsel, the better our world will be. Many have died in the pain of their marriages; many are living below their capacity and potential because their marriage has become a distraction and is draining them. Consequently, they cannot give their best in their current state and environment.

I strongly recommend that women form help and support groups to empower other women to rise and be the best version of themselves. We can bind together and be our best motivation and support. We can shine a light and beam a ray of hope and also mentor younger ladies around you to know that in all their getting, they should get wisdom and understanding to deal with the affairs of life, especially in the matters of Marriage.

God bless you